BREAK UP.
ON PURPOSE.

BREAK UP.

ON PURPOSE.

A Catalyst for Growth

JOHN KIM

HarperOne
An Imprint of HarperCollinsPublishers

BREAK UP ON PURPOSE. Copyright © 2024 by John Kim. All rights reserved. Printed in the United States of America. No part of this book may be used or reproduced in any manner whatsoever without written permission except in the case of brief quotations embodied in critical articles and reviews. For information, address HarperCollins Publishers, 195 Broadway, New York, NY 10007.

HarperCollins books may be purchased for educational, business, or sales promotional use. For information, please email the Special Markets Department at SPsales@harpercollins.com.

FIRST EDITION

Designed by Yvonne Chan

Library of Congress Cataloging-in-Publication Data has been applied for.

ISBN 978-0-06-327533-1
ISBN 978-0-06-343038-9 (Intl)

24 25 26 27 28 LBC 5 4 3 2 1

For my daughter, Logan,
because you will go through many.

Someday it's all going to make sense.

Contents

BREAK UP.
ON PURPOSE.

Introduction

When people aren't used to asking for things, they either announce it with a hard line that makes you wonder who this person is or mumble it casually under their breath like they're asking you to pass the ketchup. She did the latter.

I could tell it was hard for her. But I wasn't thinking about her. I was thinking about me, as usual. She wanted a separation, but I didn't feel the weight of what that meant because I saw this as an opportunity to finally give her something. My chance to be a man, a good husband, something I hadn't been since we'd gotten married five years ago. We were no longer young artists in Hollywood trying to make it—romantic and dreamy. She was traveling the world and working on movie sets while I was wearing dishwashing gloves, picking up dog shit, and accepting the failure of my screenwriting career. In other words, about to hit my rock bottom. Besides, it's not like she was asking for a divorce. She just needed some space. She said it would make us better, and I believed it. Got it. Heard. Done. This time, no pushback. "Whatever you need." This was my opportunity to be a better husband—a better man.

The separation request quickly turned into "Can you be out when I get home?" So I found a temporary room on Craigslist. Then, once I was out, she wanted a divorce. This time with firm lips and a hard line. It was then that I realized there was no escape plan the entire time. There was no "us" getting better. Only her getting away.

I left with nothing but my Tempur-Pedic pillow. She got the bed. I was thirty-five and starting all over. I had nothing. No money. No friends. No career. No sense of self. No direction. No idea what my life was going to look like. She had just booked a series regular on a major network that could possibly give her financial security for life. I had emotional whiplash, debt, and a new lock on my bedroom door to keep out a possessive and controlling roommate. I felt lost and left behind. Held back because I flunked love.

I didn't just lose a marriage; I lost everything that could have been: the picket fence, matching BMWs, kids, and pancakes on Sundays. Being best friends with my daughter. Family time. Soccer games. All of it, gone. The poster was ripped down overnight. Sometimes losing what could have been is more devastating than what was (more about this later). This idea of what we were building was the sun I revolved around, so when she left, my life went dark.

The good news about starting with nothing is that you have nothing to lose. And when you have nothing to lose, you have nothing to prove. You meet fear by the bikes at three o'clock because you're tired of being bullied. You don't care what people think about your life anymore because you don't have one. There's something freeing about that. You wake up alone, go to sleep alone, and have no one to answer to but yourself.

But most importantly, you start asking yourself different questions, questions you never asked when you were in a relationship. There were so many other questions that needed answering first. *Did you return the Amazon package? Can we try a different pizza place? Did you pick up the mustard? What do you want to be for Halloween because we NEED to match?*

Enter new questions. *Why am I so unhappy? Who am I and what do I want to experience in this life? How can I make an impact? What do I want to leave behind? Where is my true north, and what does it look like to start swimming in that direction? What do I truly deserve? What do I truly want? How do I want to be loved? What do I bring to the table? How do I want to show up? How can I reconnect to myself and my body? How can I start living a life that's inside out instead of outside in? How can I start attracting instead of chasing? How can my story help others?*

Searching for answers to these questions became my life rudder. Instead of sinking, I started swimming. Suddenly I was back in school studying to become a therapist. I was doing burpees and pull-ups as a daily regimen, discarding the false belief that I'm not an athlete, formed in high school while warming a bench for four years. I bought a motorcycle and hugged canyons in Malibu, connecting to the spirit of the twelve-year-old I'd been disconnected from ever since I was sporting fat laces and spinning on my head in the '80s. I started writing again—not to sell, but to share. To help others. Slowly, one day at a time, I started building a new life. But more importantly, I built a brand-new self.

That was fifteen years ago.

Today I am fifty. I have a daughter. She's four. Not into soccer, but she loves art. She has strong boundaries, and we're working on the whole "best friends" thing. And she hates pancakes. My partner is also a therapist, and we live in the Altadena Hills. Instead of a picket fence, we have an ice plunge in our driveway. No matching BMWs. I ride a Harley, and she has an electric Volvo. This family life is not the image I had when I was married. But it's everything I've ever wanted. I know because I feel it in my body and soul.

My divorce was both the hardest thing I've ever gone through *and* the single greatest event that ever happened to me. It repositioned my life, forcing me to do a self-inventory, to build and connect back to self, to find drive and purpose. In giving me not only a life but a cape (purpose), it gave me something I'd never had before.

Of course, it wasn't easy. There were days when I felt lost and hopeless. Discouraged and depressed. I spent many days alone in my room wondering if I would survive. But I took it one day at a time and started stringing days together like an addict getting sober—having mostly bad days but some good days as I slowly inched forward, trusting the process. People said there would be something on the other side. I wasn't sure I believed that, but a sliver of curiosity kept me going. I implemented structure and slowly adopted a new mindset. It took a few years, but eventually I tipped, realizing I'd swum too far to turn back. The good days started to eclipse the bad ones.

Finally, I broke through. There was no announcement. I didn't wake up one day and feel like a new person. But all these changes created a space for insights and revelations, a space where I found peace and developed an ability to like myself, to truly grieve, to seek joy instead of chasing shiny things, and eventually to create new definitions of love and life—to see the world through new lenses. I experienced secondary change, the kind that's irreversible. I evolved. Became someone different.

And my breakup was the catalyst for this change. If not for my divorce, I don't know who I would be today. Or what I would be doing with my life. I'm pretty sure I would still be a grayed-out miserable fuck going through life with white knuckles and a fixed mindset. I could finally see that my divorce, a curse at the time, was the greatest gift I ever received.

But more than growth, self-discovery, and a new life, my divorce gave me something else that is greater than me and my story. The end of that relationship offered me a chance to help others. In the past fifteen years, I've helped thousands of people with their expired relationships. People from all different walks of life, from different countries, different socioeconomic backgrounds, each going through their own unique breakup. My greatest revelation has been not only that we have to recalibrate the meaning of breakups and learn to see them as the most powerful single event that can spark growth and reposition our lives, but also that a breakup sheds light on the wounding within us that needs to be healed, and on the different types of wounds.

This revelation means that what you need to focus on to start healing from a breakup will vary, depending on the type of breakup you're going through. A blindsided breakup is very different from a mutual uncoupling where you stay friends and coparent. Each of these types of breakups produces different thoughts and feelings, so they require different plans and ways of processing. An amicable breakup will produce feelings of sadness and grief, while one resulting from infidelity will produce anger, rage, and a sense of betrayal. A mutual uncoupling is the closing of a chapter. In a blindsided breakup, you're left with a lot of questions and internalization.

It's crucial that we consider differences like these, even if the world tends to see breakups in only one color. If we don't, it's like we're going to the doctor and saying we need medication because we're sick without getting our sickness diagnosed. Your priorities differ depending on what type of breakup you're going through. For example, a toxic, chaotic breakup requires prioritizing strong boundaries, while cutting the cord may not be a priority in a mutual conscious uncoupling, but rather having an honest conversation about what being friends will look like. You will also need to process different things as you heal. To break the pattern that led to a blindsided breakup, you need to ask why you are only drawn into toxic and chaotic relationships. In a mutual uncoupling, the issue may be not expressing your needs until it's too late.

Yes, all breakups follow similar steps to healing, but depending on the type of breakup you're going through, your priorities will shift. This is the piece no one talks about. Customizing your priorities is like adjusting knobs on an equalizer to get the pitch that sounds perfect to you. This customization is what will position you for the best and most effective healing. If you don't make this adjustment, you'll be forced to listen to the same pitch as everyone else but with different ears.

We have never broken down breakups into different categories. We have broken down the ways we prefer to give and receive love, hence the five love languages. We have broken down communication styles. We have broken down attachment styles. But we have never considered different types of breakups. Most people think a breakup is just a breakup, just something "you need to get over." But discerning how and why your relationship ended is a crucial part of your healing. This is why I wrote this book. To give you a clearer road map of the specific things you need to explore and process and the action steps you need to focus on, depending on the type of breakup you're going through.

Finally, breakups linger. This is another important factor not explored or written about much. Many of my clients still struggle with the residue of a breakup that happened years ago but has impacted their inner life and relationships ever since. They keep playing back what happened, and it consumes them, preventing them from being present in their current relationship. Or they never took any accountability, so what they contributed to the breakup is now showing up in their new relationship. They never broke through to a new understanding; instead, they just moved on.

But their unacknowledged contribution to the breakup

carries over. Until they go back and truly understand what happened and what their piece in it was—taking ownership, which is what leads to closure (more about this later)—they won't heal and the breakup will continue to follow them like a dark cloud. Given that we're likely to experience at least several breakups during our lifetimes, this kind of cloud can turn into a permanent relationship storm.

My divorce was just one breakup in my life. I have been through many, from the end of long-term relationships to potent dating gone south. Each breakup was different, and none of them were easy. Like you, I've been confused and left afterward in a world of hurt. Cried orange tears from wiping them with my Cheetos-stained fingers as I ate my feelings and drowned in what-ifs on Friday nights, wondering if I would ever find love again.

I've also hurt others. I've left relationships without really working on them. Experienced guilt and shame and wondered if I made the right decision. I've spent years spinning in my head and heart after a breakup, wishing things had played out differently, waiting for emails of apology and explanations that would prove I was not crazy. They never came. Like so many, I hit pause on dating or wasn't present in relationships because I didn't have "closure" on previous ones.

But through it all, I've healed and learned, snapped back, healed and learned, and so on, turning my breakups into break-throughs as I continue to rediscover myself and form new definitions of love.

Here's what no one wants to hear. Breakups are a natural, normal part of life. They are unavoidable, like puberty and crooked teeth. If you choose to love in this world, you will go through a breakup, most likely many breakups. And it may be hard to hear right now, but you're meant to go through what you're going through. Because nothing will transform you more than the healing of a broken heart. It's a healing that creates the richest soil for growth.

Many see their breakup as a horrific life event, like a car accident that leaves you crippled, or the sudden, unexpected death of a loved one you don't think you can live without. Like being wrongfully accused and terminated at your dream job pursuing a career you've worked your entire life for. Yes, a breakup may feel catastrophic, but the truth is that breakups are a rite of passage. Under the pain are dots you will be able to connect later, after the emotional dust settles and you have new lenses and sharper clarity. Through this journey, you will build a healthier version of yourself and learn what it takes to give yourself a new love experience. And it's in *this* new experience that bodies are rewired, trauma is worked through, false beliefs are dissolved, the self is better understood, and new definitions and standards are created. All these are steps that contribute to our evolution. Our breakups are actually how we grow.

So, take a deep breath.
The deepest breath you've taken in a long time.
And as you exhale, notice the sensations in your body.

The tension in your neck. The knots in your shoulders. The twist in your stomach. All your spinning thoughts.

Take another deep breath and as you exhale, see the tension untangling.

The thoughts dissolving.

The anxiety releasing.

Your shoulders dropping.

Take another deep breath.

Exhale.

Untangle.

Dissolve.

Release.

Say to yourself:

There was a reason.

And as I heal,

I will discover the gift in all of this.

HOW THIS BOOK WORKS

This book has three pistons:

Real-life client stories: Because stories are how we relate, learn, and feel less alone, they are required for anyone going through a breakup.

"What Really Happened": Investigating in each of these stories why the plane went down, we come to a better understanding of the self and take ownership of the need to

change our love patterns. This is a necessary step if we are to eventually give ourselves a new love experience.

"Break-Through Work": Although the steps in this book pertain to all breakups, because you'll prioritize and focus on different things depending on the kind of breakup you're going through, "Break-Through Work" is customized to fit specific types of breakups.

These three pistons pumping together will move you forward and keep you on track in your healing journey.

Let's break it down.

The (anonymous) client stories are real-life examples of seven different types of breakups. There is healing power in hearing the stories of others. You feel like you're not the only one going through a breakup. Others have been there. Some even had it worse. When you're going through a breakup, it's crucial to not feel alone. We can isolate and fall into a depression when we feel alone. These stories make what you're going through an "us" thing instead of a "you" thing. Each story is unique, entering through a different door as it demonstrates one type of breakup. But all the stories, though they are wildly different, contain common themes we can all relate to.

After each story is a section titled "What Really Happened." Figuring out what happened is an essential part of healing from a breakup. Because most of us were never taught how to look deeper, too often we just stay with the surface explanation for what went wrong and our wounds never really heal. We gain no insights or revelations, so we continue to cast blame and to believe we're victims. Instead of seeking closure and then moving on with more wisdom and insight, with more compassion and expansive hearts, we just focus on forgetting. But forgetting isn't healing. Healing happens through learning what happened, processing feelings, and changing yourself through the actions you take.

Many of us don't find peace after a breakup because we never try to discover what *really* happened. We just react to our feelings and constantly play back a story that isn't true. This is how we get stuck. Without bringing fresh lenses to an honest investigation, we're left with foggy understanding, rumination, and overthinking. Gaining clarity about what truly happened allows us to process the emotions associated with the breakup and start to move through it. Feelings are validated as we go through the stages of grief.

As these client stories demonstrate, investigating what really happened in a breakup enriches the soil for accepting it. After each story, I explain what really happened in the relationship so you can start to explore what happened in yours.

The final part of this book is the "Break-Through Work." I have found that my clients actually want a to-do list of action steps they can implement. They don't want to just process their feelings. They need a road map. Many times when you're going through a breakup, you don't trust yourself. You need handrails. That's what the "Break-Through Work" will give you: practical, street-level steps to get you out of the trenches and back into your life.

Before we begin, I want to remind you of two misconceptions about breakups. One, your heart didn't actually break. And two, it's okay to numb away. Let me explain.

YOUR HEART DIDN'T BREAK

One of the greatest misconceptions about breakups is that they leave you broken. Injured. Clipped and defective. Your heart has shattered, and it's going to take a lifetime to put it back together again. Yes, it may feel that way. But the truth is, our hearts don't break. They stretch. And this stretching of the heart is what creates a greater capacity to love.

Heartbreak is a natural part of life that can take various forms. We can experience heartbreak not just in romantic relationships but also in friendships, in our family dynamics, and through other personal connections. When relationships end, we investigate and learn more about ourselves, our thinking and behavior, and where it all came from. This investigation helps us throw out old blueprints we may still be tracing and gives us an opportunity to reevaluate our beliefs and what we truly want for ourselves. This is why I say a breakup creates the richest soil for growth.

Heartbreak teaches us important lessons about ourselves and others. It helps us understand our own boundaries, desires, and needs. It shows us what we truly value in relationships and what we are willing to accept or let go of. Through heartbreak, we learn about resilience, self-reflection, and inner growth. Heartbreak highlights our connection to self, and this connection repositions us. Not just with love, but with life. It allows us to let go of what no longer serves us and to make space for new experiences. It teaches us to be more compassionate, toward both ourselves and others, as we navigate the complexities of love and relationships.

A heartbreak can be the catalyst to reevaluate your entire life. For example, most people who go through a divorce (including myself) shake up their Life-Etch-A-Sketch—they do a complete life inventory. They examine all areas of their lives. They change careers. They make new friends and shed old ones who'd just been hanging on because of history. They move across the country and adopt completely new lifestyles. They pursue new hobbies and interests, pick up weights as well as guitars, and take salsa classes again. They write that book they've always wanted to write. They buy motorcycles, climb mountains, and work on their bodies. They explore their sexuality and different relationship models. Basically, they un-pause their life and start to live again. Or maybe they start living for the first time.

A breakup isn't just a chapter in your life. It can be a break between acts. A total repositioning. There may be a totally new life waiting for you when you realize it wasn't your heart that broke. It was your unhealthy love patterns, your faulty way of thinking, the hold that patriarchy has had on you. It was your tolerance for staying in something that wasn't honest. What broke was your silence.

Your heart is not broken. Because hearts don't break. They stretch. In order to love harder and deeper. Softer and wiser.

You are not getting over anyone.

You are becoming.

You are evolving.
Your heart didn't break.
It awakened.

Your breakup is a rite of passage. But you are not going through it. It is going through you.

Now what will you do with your awakened heart? How will you show up differently and how will that ripple outward? How will your life change because of this awakening? How will that impact others? How will that prove that what you went through or are currently going through is greater than you?

IT'S OKAY TO NUMB AWAY (CONSCIOUSLY)

The pain of heartbreak can be one of the most excruciating emotional experiences a person goes through in their lifetime. We actually feel physical pain (studies show that heartbreak activates the same part of our brain activated by physical pain), and we struggle to eat, sleep, and focus. Grief actually mimics depression, so while we're healing we can also experience legit depression.

In addition to grieving the loss of both our partner and our imagined future, our self-worth usually takes a massive hit—because, well, #rejection. If the person who loved you the most suddenly decides they don't love you or want to be with you anymore, how are you supposed to feel? Of course you're going to assume it was something about you that led them to that decision. Maybe you play a common track from your story—from your upbringing—that it was about your not being good enough. So you've got grief and rejection both, a one-two punch. But wait! There's more.

Breakups can activate our stored trauma. If we have any type of abandonment wound (for example, if we experienced physical or emotional abandonment by a parent through divorce, death, mental illness, addiction, or poverty), a breakup can make us feel like we're that helpless child all over again. This is why sometimes when we're ugly-crying on the floor, our tears can feel "old"—as though we're crying about something deeper than the breakup itself. This is also why the pain of a breakup can send us into a state of panic and leave us feeling like we're dying: the wounds stored deep in our unconscious are exposed, and we think that in order to survive we need to cling to our partner. In those moments, it's important to remind ourselves that we're adults who can and will survive (and eventually thrive) without our exes.

Picture your breakup as a pie chart. At first, all it serves up is pain or distraction. You're either deep in the feelings or you're numbing yourself with the wine or the weed or the rebound. Over time, though, you start to enjoy moments (little pie pieces) when you can actually be present with neither pain nor distraction. This is how you know that you're moving through your breakup. Or rather, that your breakup is moving through you (as I'll explain later). You might not call these moments "happy" just yet, but they no longer feel either excruciating or numbing. Still, until we get to the place in our healing where we experience more slices of those "relief" moments, we have to give ourselves permission to distract and numb ourselves as needed.

In our self-help culture, we say we should "feel to heal." This is absolutely true, but with breakups we just can't "feel" all the time. And if we're into personal growth and want to do the breakup "right," we tend to judge ourselves for distracting ourselves or numbing. At this point, not only are we in pain, but we feel shame—over feeling like we're sabotaging or delaying our healing process. So here's my advice to you: First, reframe "numbing" as "coping," as "surviving." Because that's what you need to focus on right now. Just fucking surviving. Then ask yourself what survival strategies you can give yourself permission to use without shame.

For a while during my last breakup, I had an edible every night for weeks. Every night. One result was that I sent a few incoherent emails to my ex, but otherwise it helped me cope with some super-lonely evenings and get some much-needed sleep. I'm not saying you should go out and buy some edibles, or otherwise use your breakup as an opportunity to find a new addiction. But if you need to throw some less-than-perfect coping into your heartbreak recovery plan, welcome to being human.

Whatever your coping strategy, just be intentional about it. Make the decision to "consciously numb" without judging yourself for it. Most importantly, see your coping as temporary. If you're still bingeing every night or spending every weekend in bed marathoning Netflix three months out, you might want to have some honest words with yourself (or your therapist).

Okay, now let's begin your journey.

THE EIGHT TYPES OF BREAKUPS

Over the years I've helped clients with their breakups, I've discovered that most of them fall into one of eight categories. Like love languages, there may be elements from more than one of these types in your breakup, but one of them will fit your situation the best. You will be able to say, "Yes, this is the type of breakup I'm going through." Also, one type of breakup can turn into another type of breakup, and so your plan to heal will change according to the type you're going through. I get into more detail about how to handle each type of breakup later. For now, the broad strokes.

The "Big One"—The First True Love Breakup

Everyone has their "big one." The one we compare all other relationships and breakups to because it was the first imprint. Usually this was our first true love—and by "true love" I mean (most likely) an unhealthy love, maybe during college or in our twenties. The kind of love we lost ourselves in because we didn't have a sense of self and our hearts were fresh powdered snow. It was intense because we didn't know how to love. We just went with what we felt, creating a steep cliff that eventually we fell over, hard.

The "big one" can also be a relationship that happened later in life, depending on your relationship history. For example, the "big one" for me wasn't my first relationship. It was my marriage when I was in my thirties. What's challenging about the "big one" isn't necessarily healing from the breakup but rather having it continue to haunt you. It carries over. It follows you for many, many years—decades for some. And it impacts other relationships.

The Blindsided Breakup

They say you never *don't* know. Yes, sleeping in separate rooms for the last two years may be an obvious sign that your relationship has been in trouble. But the actual breakup can feel like it came out of nowhere, without any warning. That's because most of us avoid conflict, push things down, compartmentalize, and ignore problems. We get used to the bad until the bad becomes the norm. When that homeostasis bursts, the breakup, shocking and sometimes even traumatic, can feel like it came out of nowhere.

The challenging thing about this type of breakup is coping with the lack of prep time. Your life can change overnight without warning. One day you're in a relationship, partnership, or marriage, and the next day you're not. For some people, a blindsided breakup can trigger reactions that cause them to spiral. This type of breakup is less about the loss and more about the ripple of the shock.

The Flat Soda Breakup:
"We Should Have Broken Up Years Ago"

This breakup is the cleanest type of breakup. Since both you and your partner are on the same page and your feelings are mutual, neither of you has to protect the other. There is no drama. Or at least, there's a lot less. There's usually no guilt, no sense that either of you did something wrong.

There's only grieving and sadness. That doesn't necessarily make it easier to get through than the other types of breakups. In fact, sometimes it's easier to be angry than sad. But a flat soda breakup can be less complicated than the other types. You don't have to look over your shoulder or live in a panic state. Boundaries are mutually drawn and respected. Since you don't have feelings for each other anymore, you experience fewer reactions to the breakup, and less jealousy. You may be leaving some issues unresolved, but generally you want the best for each other.

This breakup ends with a handshake, not a knife in the back. But unlike the other breakups, the flat soda breakup can produce the most regret. You may be mad at yourself for not ending it sooner, or you may feel bad for holding your partner hostage.

The "You Cheated/Left Me for Someone Else" Breakup

What's difficult about the "you cheated/left me for someone else" breakup is the internalization. It's not just that you were betrayed. It's believing that you are less than, or defective, because your partner was unfaithful.

The truth is, infidelity is complicated and involves so many factors and layers we don't explore, investigate, or process. We just point fingers and default to victim mode. This black-and-white thinking turns us into cardboard cutouts and prevents us from truly healing and moving on. We become angry and untrusting. We love behind plexiglass from then on, because the love stove will always be too hot to touch.

The Soap Opera Breakup: "I Need to Get a Restraining Order"

The soap opera breakup delivers a one-two punch. Not only are you dealing with the chaotic turmoil of a relationship that's ending, but you may also have to protect yourself to ensure your mental, emotional, and sometimes physical safety. Usually, the more chaotic the breakup is, the more unhealthy the relationship was, but that is not always the case. High emotions can cause people to act in ways they normally wouldn't.

One factor contributing to a soap opera breakup is how the relationship ended. For example, a blindsided breakup can turn into a chaotic breakup. Or a divorce can turn ugly when the spouses start fighting over money or custody. Either way, when a breakup turns into this type of breakup, you are in self-protecting fight-or-flight mode. Your priority is protecting yourself, your workspace, your home, and your life. For a while, healing has to take a backseat.

The Almost-Relationship Breakup

As I mentioned in my own story, the breakup with my wife wasn't just about losing a marriage. It was about losing the vivid glossy-poster image of what could have been, the future and the family life I could have had with her. Fantasizing about wrestling with your daughter and making pancakes on Sundays can get you believing there's more to this image than there actually is.

You don't have to be married to experience this kind of loss. It can even happen when you're dating. We fill in blanks fast, creating the kind of fantasy future with someone that we've been wanting for a very long time. Losing that can be crushing. This is why many underestimate the impact of the breakup of an almost-relationship. We believe that since it never turned into a full, "real" relationship, we shouldn't be crushed when it ends. That we should "get over it" quickly. But intensity is not tied to time. And sometimes the ending of an almost-relationship can be more heartbreaking than breaking up a long-term relationship. Hope is a real thing. So is future tripping.

The Breakup That Never Ends

We've all done this. We've said it was over and then, at a coffee catch-up a few months later, glimpsed new possibilities as we both subtly brag about how much we've grown and changed and what we learned about ourselves and about love through our relationship. Missing each other puts us on our best behavior, puts us back in alignment, and reignites the spark we felt when we first met—before the disagreements, before the constant defensiveness, before the missed anniversaries, hurtful words, and resentment.

But the thing is, it's all still there. Right underneath the highlight reel and the forgiving smiles. And so it begins again. Round two. Then the realization hits that nothing's changed. Some time goes by. Then we go another round. And another . . .

The D Word—Divorce

A divorce has many more layers than the other types of breakups. You may have children and own property together, maybe even a family business. You're not just breaking up. You're distributing lamps. Agreeing on custody. Negotiating alimony, child support, and coparenting. And losing in-laws, family members, and dividing friends.

Many who get divorced can't just leave and start over wherever they want. Most have to still see and communicate with each other, have to change their relationship from romantic to platonic, because they are still tied to their ex in some way—as business partners or as coparents if they're raising children. This is not an easy thing to do, especially if one spouse didn't want to divorce. Because divorces are not just about love but about lives, they can turn ugly very fast. There's more at stake in this type of breakup than in any other. And when there's more at stake, there is more to work through.

You may have the urge to skip to the chapter on the specific type of breakup you're going through. But I encourage you to read through all of them in the order they're written. You will relate to the discussion of each type on some level. If it doesn't relate to the breakup you're going through now, it may resonate with a past breakup that's impacting you today and how you show up in relationships. You may have not even been aware of that until you read about how that happens.

Relationships end in different ways, but you will find common themes in all the breakups and client stories recounted in this book. Themes that create rich soil for revelations and insights—for break-throughs.

The "Big One"—
The First True Love Breakup

There are all kinds of love in this world.
But never the same love twice.

—F. SCOTT FITZGERALD

JESS AND BRIAN

Brian was two years older than Jess. At their tiny college, it was almost absurd that she somehow had never seen him before. She for sure would have remembered him.

On the day they were supposed to leave on a spring break trip for Habitat for Humanity, Jess walked up to the van hungover and foggy-eyed from three hours of sleep and far too much Carlo Rossi wine the night before. She nearly fainted when Brian came rushing over to introduce himself.

He was six-foot-two, Hispanic, with light eyes and a million-watt smile that could melt snow.

Holyyyy shit, Jess thought as she stumbled through her introduction. *I'm in trouble. Capital T trouble.*

And so they began a twenty-one-hour drive. Students rotated seats and drivers almost every time they stopped for gas or a bathroom break or snacks. They stopped at old diners. Someone found a bra stuffed into the cushions of their booth. The group sang songs, told stories. Everyone laughed. Brian bounced around and talked to everyone. To Jess, he was sparkling, magical. The groups for the trip had been randomly assigned, so most of them didn't know each other. They asked each other what felt to nineteen- and twenty-year-olds like deep questions: "What's your life story?" "Are you happy?"

Jess fell asleep in the front seat in the middle of a sentence, though her job had been to keep talking to keep the driver awake. Another student soon ousted her and sent her to the middle-row middle seat—the worst seat in the van, the seat of shame.

But Jess was not sad about it, because now she was sitting next to Brian, who soon fell asleep too. For a magical thirty-minute stretch, he slept on her shoulder, soft dark curls on her cheek. Though she had just been falling asleep herself, Jess was suddenly wide awake and buzzing. She had to remind herself to breathe. When he woke with a start, laughing, he slapped her knee and told her about a dream that he was falling off a cliff.

"Oh," Jess said, remembering to exhale, "I know the feeling."

When the van arrived in Arizona, everyone was bleary-eyed and delirious. It had been arranged for them to sleep in an old church—all of them lined up next to each other in sleeping bags on the floor of what usually was a rec room. Zero privacy in a church space ensured that nothing too interesting happened, despite the proximity and lack of supervision.

The next day they set out for the construction site. Though the group had been together only a day and a half, little cliques had already started to form. Like any social group, they organized themselves roughly according to the *Breakfast Club* model—brains, athletes, basket cases, princesses, and bad boys. Just as quickly, Jess's crush on Brian took a turn for the tragic. Assuming that there was no way he would ever look twice at a girl like her (more basket case than princess), Jess had decided that another girl on the trip, Heidi (all princess), was obviously the love of his life. Heidi was a sporty hiker with blond hair and dimples. She was sweet and wholesome, looked adorable in a baseball cap, and dressed like she had walked out of an REI catalog, in hiking boots and perfectly coordinated olive green gear with a matching backpack. Jess wore an old sweatshirt, worn-out bell bottom jeans with flower patches, and a red bandana. As for the dimpled wholesomeness, Jess did not have even one cute dimple, and frankly, she swore far too much to be sleeping in a church. Brian and Heidi obviously had tons in common and would look great together. He even seemed to be avoiding Jess a little bit, so *clearly* he was in love with Heidi.

By the second night of the trip, Jess had pretty comfortably resigned herself to unrequited love. But Brian always sat next to her at meals, often finding excuses to touch her leg or arm while talking, and sometimes he pulled her bandanna off and wore it himself. Clearly, he had taken Jess under his wing as a little sister. She was happy for the camaraderie, and he made her laugh.

On the final night of the trip, at a bonfire, Brian tried to get a sing-along started. He played guitar to popular folk songs from the '70s and waited for everyone to join in—but Jess was the only one who knew all the words. They ended up facing each other, playing and singing more to each other than to anyone else and sort of forgetting that everyone else was there. That night he snuck his sleeping bag next to hers, and they stayed up half the night talking and trying not to laugh loud enough to wake anyone else up.

Jess was still entirely convinced that Brian and Heidi would end up together, have kids, and go hiking in their perfectly coordinated gear and ridiculous diamond-sparkling smiles. So she was completely taken off guard on the last day of the trip when Brian hung his head while they walked on the beach and sheepishly asked if she was planning to ever hang out with him when they got back to campus.

What?" Jess asked, completely flummoxed. Did she miss something? Was this a joke?

Brian grabbed Jess's hand.

"I really like you. Obviously. I just haven't figured out how to ask you if you have a boyfriend. I tried to ask PJ but he didn't know, and Sam thought you were dating a med school student but you haven't mentioned him, and then PJ said I should just go for it and kiss you, but I didn't want to just do that and then get rejected, and so . . ."

"Wait. Hold on," Jess said. "You like *me*? I thought . . . I thought, maybe you and Heidi?"

His warm hand in hers had turned her blood into molasses, and everything felt like it was going in slow motion.

Brian stopped being sheepish and started laughing.

"Heidi?! Oh God, she's just so boring." More laughing. "I mean, don't get me wrong, she's a sweet girl, but there is nothing there behind those eyes, no-thing. We don't have anything in common at all, she's so hard to talk to. Me and Heidi? That's a laugh."

He wasn't avoiding her because he didn't like her. He was avoiding her because he did.

How very strange.

Before Jess could tell Brian that she liked him too, that she wanted him to kiss her more than maybe anything else on earth, Sam came running down the beach yelling, "Guys, we're going to miss the bus! It's our last night! Come on!"

They turned and ran back toward the parking lot, still hand in hand.

"You still didn't answer me, Ace." Yes, he called her Ace. "You gonna hang out with me when we get back to campus?"

Jess played it cool, but not too cool for him to stop.

"Well, duh." Still reeling in disbelief over her luck.

Brian liked her. Jess thought: *I'm not sure if anyone has created a hierarchy of different kinds of love ranked from the kind that makes you the most irrational to the least, but they should. For sure at the top of the pyramid—the kind of love that makes you the most completely irrational and insane—would be the kind where you have completely resigned yourself to loving someone from afar and it turns out they love you back. I'm pretty sure that it's such whiplash that all your rational brain cells go shooting out of your ears as your head spins.*

Just like that, Jess fell in love.

Uncharacteristically, she found herself spilling her guts to the girls in the bathroom while they got ready for the night out.

"Does anyone have a jean jacket I could borrow? Should I wear my hair up or down? Or—wait, wait, wait—half up?"

Brian and Jess sat next to each other at dinner and got tipsy. They danced at a salsa club and snuck out onto a rickety wooden stairway behind some bar to make out. In the most romantic gesture to date, Brian held Jess's face, looked deep into her eyes, and said he loved her.

Over the next three months, back at school, Jess became someone else entirely, someone she used to roll her eyes at. Someone she used to be disappointed in. Jess cried on nights when Brian didn't call. She ditched her friends when Brian *did* call. She watched movies that she had no interest in. She ate food she didn't like, drank beer that she thought tasted like garbage, and pretended to be super into bands that she hated.

Jess was nervous all the time—probably because she was faking everything. She wore clothes that she thought Brian liked. She went camping even though she didn't like sleeping outside, read books she wasn't interested in, and agreed with arguments that she actually disagreed with. Jess ignored red flags and refused to listen to her friends when they pointed out how arrogant Brian could be, a little mean even. There was a quiet voice inside her wondering how he could fall "in love" with her so fast. But she shut that voice down real quick. Worst of all, Jess didn't listen to her dad, who thought Brian was completely and entirely full of shit behind that glittering smile.

The point of this story is not to label Brian an asshole. After all, he was nineteen and cocky and probably unsure and confused behind that cockiness—like we all were at nineteen. This is a story about how Jess gave herself up. It is a story about how much you can learn about yourself when you act like a complete idiot. This is a story about young love—love that comes along when our hearts are fresh and raw and trusting because we haven't been hurt before.

How quickly we can lose all the best things about ourselves when we believe our feelings are facts. We have many more heartbreaks to go through before realizing that a relationship like Jess and Brian's is not a relationship between two people—it's a relationship between a half-person and an ideal. The other person becomes a temple we worship, and we become a half-person in our worship of them. We don't see them for who they are, and we make it impossible for them to see us for who we are ourselves.

The night it all unraveled, Jess had gotten ready early and was waiting for the phone to ring. While she listened to sad music in her dorm, all dressed up to go out, she drank a couple of beers by herself. Brian finally reached out around eight: "We're partying at my house, Ace. Come over if you want." She practically ran to Brian's off-campus house in her espadrilles, which she had bought to remind him of the magic of the first night they kissed. He had been distant all week and flaked on plans the night before. Jess was tense and frantic, determined not to lose him.

When she got to his house, it was clear that the party had been going on for a couple of hours. Brian waved to her from across the room when he saw her, gave her a terse smile and a head nod, and then continued his conversation with his friends. He didn't come over to give her a hug, didn't wave her over to join them.

Jess tried to make conversation with other people at the party, to show him that she was still fun, but it wasn't working. He barely said hello to her and had his back to her most of the night. Through boozy spiraling thoughts, Jess suddenly remembered laughing with him about his crazy ex-girlfriend, who had shown up absolutely hammered one night after he had tried to break up with her. When he hid in his bedroom to escape the drama, she banged on it with her fists, screaming like a banshee, and had to be carried off by a couple of the guys.

Jess tried to steel herself. She would not be that crazy girl, drunk and yelling at someone who was clearly no longer interested. *He loves you*, she tried to remind herself. *He's in love with you. It's going to be fine.*

It was not going to be fine.

Jess tried flirting with some of his friends. They got weirded out, and Brian didn't even notice. She tried laughing and pretending to be having such an interesting conversation that he would want to join. He didn't notice. She tried dropping things and bending over in front of him. He didn't notice.

A couple more drinks later, when she was even less rational than she'd started out, Jess decided that the best and only remaining option was seduction. *If we could just have one night of mind-blowing sex*, she thought, *he'll snap back into being in love with me.*

It was very late at night by then, and the party was dwindling. Brian was in a corner of the living room with his guitar, and Jess was too drunk to get there in a straight line. In a zigzagging sort of saunter, Jess crossed the room and stopped in front of Brian. In front of all his roommates and the rest of the party stragglers, she drunkenly swung one espadrille-clad foot over his thigh, and then the other, in an attempt to straddle him in his chair while he was still holding his guitar.

"Um, hey, what are you doing, Ace?"

She didn't know how to say, *Giving you my body for a receipt, proof you are interested in me.*

So she casually flirted: "We should . . . I'm good for tonight."

He stared at her as if he'd been waiting for this all night. "Good for what?"

She winked with the wrong eye. "You know."

But his words didn't match his expression. "I think you've maybe had too much."

He started peeling one of her legs off of him. He didn't want to have sex. Not with her, anyway. Jess turned red, horrified at the rejection. The public rejection. She fled across the living room, knocking over glasses, trying to stay upright. She barreled outside, slamming the door so hard the windows shook.

Jess set off running and kept running—and crying—all the way down the street and back to the dorms—in the middle of winter, in a tank top and fucking espadrilles, and because she was seventeen drinks in, she twisted her ankle and fell more than once. By the time she got back to the dorm, she had bloody palms and mascara running down her face. She had to get inside but couldn't face going back to her room yet—where she'd wake up roommates who would be clambering over each other to be the first to say "I told you so!"

So Jess climbed up to the top stairwell, where no one would walk by or hear her, and she cried. And cried and cried and cried. She cried so much her nose started to bleed, which she didn't notice until drops of blood dripped onto the white tile stairway. That was it. Her life was over. Nothing else mattered as she stared at the blood from her nose on the floor.

Plop, plop, plop.

She woke up the next day in the same spot. It looked like a murder scene. Her mascara smeared, blood all over her shirt and the floor. Jess had never felt so alone, or so embarrassed.

How did she get here? Just a few months earlier, she'd been able to see through anyone's curls and sparkling smile. She realized it was time for her to take the advice that she had often given her roommates and girlfriends. She'd told them, stop crying over a mediocre dude and go live your life.

Get back to yourself. Remember who you are. If you miss him, distract yourself. Go find someone new to crush on. Pick up a new hobby. Throw yourself into your work. Give it a little time and you'll get some perspective. You'll look back and laugh at how upset you got over this silliness.

But those were just thoughts. It wasn't how Jess felt. She felt like her heart had been ripped out of her chest. Which was why it seemed to so logically follow that she didn't have a heart anymore. It was in a jar with the others on Brian's shelf. He was a collector. And she should have known.

There was a Habitat for Humanity information meeting a couple of weeks later, and program veterans were asked to come speak to interested students about what it was like. The little group would be reunited, and it was the first time Jess was going to see Brian since he had rejected her.

When Jess walked into the gym, she saw Sam first and went up to hug her and say hi. A few minutes into chatting, Jess noticed that Sam was making a weird face.

"What's wrong?" she asked.

Sam pointed to something behind Jess's shoulder. Jess turned around just in time to catch Brian's gaze as he playfully grabbed Heidi's baseball cap and put it on his head. Heidi laughed.

A few weeks went by and Jess did a pretty good job of forgetting about Brian and getting her life back on track. She even finished her applications for the internships she had been trying to land. She'd been putting it off since she met Brian, wanting to wait to see where he was going. Now she couldn't believe she'd been about to make a big life decision based on a boy. It was almost like she'd been possessed. *Thank God that's over*, she thought. *Never again.*

WHAT REALLY HAPPENED

Jess knew from day one what kind of person Brian was. She knew he was inconsistent, misleading, and very aware of his looks and the attention he got from women. Jess was not naive. She'd seen the red flags, but her determination not to lose him muddied her instincts and common sense.

As always happens with first loves like Jess's, she had felt a strong underlying tug telling her that if she could get him, then she had value. We often tie love to our worth, especially when we're young. Jess was a "secure" person only because she didn't actually think she had a chance with the prom king. But seeing that she *did* have a chance moved her self-worth chips from herself to this new person. Brian had leverage now. Or at least fantasy Brian—the poster image version of him—had leverage. Jess became obsessed with the image of what could be instead of seeing what truly was.

This is how we slowly lose ourselves in a first love—often when we're young but also when we're older. Sometimes the tug is even stronger later in life, especially if we've accomplished many of our goals and the only thing missing in our lives is love. The internal ticking clock becomes deafening as we get desperate and start doing things we always promised we wouldn't. Our friends see what we're doing, but we don't. The more ambivalent and wishy-washy our crush is, the more we hold on and try to convince them and control the outcome. We minimize the bad and amplify the possibilities. Hope is still ripe and hasn't hardened yet.

Pursuing impossible love doesn't make us crazy. It makes us human. And it's not just trauma bonds that we mistake for love attraction. We all want things we can't have. We all chase poster images of love objects and tie love to our worth to a certain extent. When we're close to getting what we want, we don't let go. We hang on. Tight.

To what could be.

Jess hung on.

Hoping that Brian would come around.

That he would commit to her.

That she could finally prove she was lovable.

BREAK-THROUGH WORK
Young Love Creates the Deepest Imprints

While reading Jess's story, did you think to yourself, *How could she fall so hard and fast?* Did the details of the story remind you of how you felt when you first had your heart truly broken? When your first major crush molded you like putty. When the breakup turned a magical summer into a long dark winter you didn't think you could survive. When love was everything and you thought the two of you were invincible and couldn't fail. When being the chosen one gave you life. And being ignored killed you.

That's why you remember every detail like it happened yesterday. But doesn't looking back also make you realize how far you've come? How much you've grown and evolved? Like visiting your middle school and noticing how tiny the chairs are. You quickly realize how small you were then, when it all felt so big. That's because you experienced it through young eyes, fresh eyes.

It's the same with relationships. We play back the movie of how we saw it then, not how we see it today. So the feeling produced is still grand and overwhelming. This view of the past can keep us stuck. Because it's not truth. It's trauma. Witnessed through innocent eyes that knew nothing else, that had no other experience to compare it to. What lingers in our memories is not an accurate photograph of what happened but a caricature of it. We peel scabs from our younger self. Our feelings come from who we were then, not who we are today.

The "big one"—usually the love we experienced in college or in our twenties—usually makes the deepest imprint. Yes, that may be partly because the relationship was toxic and unhealthy, which we will get into later. But that also happens because you had fewer love experiences with which to compare it. The canvas of your heart was cleaner, so every brushstroke was seen and felt. And when you play back that relationship, you see and experience it through the eyes of that younger person. Not the eyes of who you are now.

This is why some of our early breakups are the hardest to let go of. The emotional grooves are deep because you are not seeing the relationship from your perspective today— after the crash, after gaining revelations, insights, wisdom, and new definitions. You are seeing it as you were at the time, overcome by the panic, desperation, and life-or-death stakes. But because you measure that first relationship by the same measure you use for all the relationships that came after, you think it meant more than it actually did. Simply put, if the person you are now were to go back to that relationship, the feelings wouldn't be as powerful and meaningful as the feelings you're playing back. Because you would be able to see the holes you couldn't see then.

What if Your First "Big One" Keeps Haunting You?

Many people get stuck and can't move on from the "big one." Because they keep playing it back, over and over, they can't show up as their true self and be present in new relationships. They fall into the trap of comparison because they can't forget what they felt. They compare what they're feeling now—or not feeling—to what they felt then.

If this sounds familiar, remember that those feelings came from a different, younger version of you that needed to prove you were lovable, wanted, of value. You're not considering who you were then and what you didn't know. Do you still play back the "big one"? Do you find yourself comparing young love to new love and wondering why it doesn't feel as powerful? Is it difficult to stay present in a current relationship or with someone you're dating?

If your first "big one" breakup keeps haunting you, the following four journaling prompts may help you revisit and process what happened so you can move through it. Write on each of these prompts. Remember, journaling is a personal and introspective practice, so write freely, without judgment. There is no perfect length. Your entries can be as long or as short as you like. Just make sure they're honest. Don't rush. Give yourself time to sit down and write like no one's ever going to read it. *Journaling is for you.* Not for anyone else.

As you journal, you will have revelations and insights. That will begin to clear your lenses. The goal is to separate fantasy (what you felt) from reality (what is truth today).

Reflect on the relationship: Write about the positive aspects of the relationship, the lessons you learned, and the growth you experienced. Explore any underlying patterns or dynamics. What was the tug that was fueling the attraction and that you may not have been aware of? Was it tied to any false beliefs about yourself (for example, "I'm not lovable") and your story? Don't judge feelings or thoughts as they arise. Just write them down.

Express your emotions: Allow yourself to freely express your feelings about the relationship and the breakup. Write about your sadness, anger, confusion, or any other emotion you're experiencing. Give yourself permission to be honest and raw in your writing. Don't hold back.

Identify self-discoveries: Explore the ways in which this breakup led to self-discovery. What did you learn about yourself during the breakup? How are you different today? Do you have new definitions of love, dating, and relationships? Have you discovered or rediscovered any personal strengths or qualities?

Play it out: Imagine how you think the relationship would have gone if you hadn't broken up. Knowing what you know today about love and relationships, write down how it would have played out. How would it have unfolded? What problems would have persisted? How would you both have handled conflict? What would it have been like after the honeymoon phase? What are your thoughts on how you see it unfolding if it had lasted?

Be aware of how often you think about the "big one" and how it impacts you and your relationships. How does it keep you from full loving? What would it look like to close that chapter of your life? To fully let go of it?

Know that if you went back to that relationship now, you would have a very different experience. When you reminisce, you are playing back what you experienced through the lenses of your younger self. What you see is a distortion, not truth. You are remembering what you felt. Not what it actually was. Read that again.

When you fall in love, your brain undergoes a complex series of changes. The brain regions associated with reward, pleasure, and motivation become highly active, releasing chemicals like dopamine, oxytocin, and serotonin. These neurotransmitters cause feelings of euphoria, attachment, and a desire to be close to the person you're in love with. Activity in the prefrontal cortex, which is responsible for decision-making and critical thinking, might also decrease, putting you in a "lovestruck" state that keeps you from seeing your partner's flaws as readily.

Connections Are Meant to Be Played Out

Your own experience of a version of Jess's story may not have been in your twenties. Maybe the "big one" happened last summer when you turned forty. The "big one" isn't always young love. Some of us may have had crushes, but our first real love experience came later in life. And maybe it wasn't chaotic and toxic, like most young love, but actually healthy, and that's why it's so difficult to let go of it. It doesn't matter why. What matters is that it was "big"—it punctured your soul and still impacts you today. Even though the relationship didn't work out, you keep going there, obsessing over the feeling and fantasy of what could have been.

Maybe you had a knowing that the relationship was a bad idea but invested in it anyway; your friends, even your therapist perhaps, probably reminded you that you saw the end coming. Even if it wasn't clear, you felt this was a cul-de-sac. You had a feeling. Deep down inside you knew and even saw red flags, but you kept going. Or maybe you saw only green flags, but other things didn't line up and the relationship went south. Maybe it was your partner, not you, but you made excuses. Or you reframed the relationship in a way that gave you permission to hang on. Or maybe you didn't want to investigate or look deeper because you weren't ready to. Or maybe you didn't want to face your wounds and demons. No matter what . . .

IT'S OKAY.

IT'S OKAY.

IT'S OKAY.

Part of letting go is practicing self-compassion and for-giveness. I blame myself often for how I showed up (or didn't) in my "big one," but self-blame also keeps me stuck in that story. By blaming yourself you are holding on. By giving yourself grace and knowing you loved to the best of your capacity from where you were at that time in your life, you can start to release the anchor of self-blame. Know that you did your best. You didn't have the awareness or tools then. Be kind to yourself. The more you blame yourself for what happened, the tighter the grip the event has on you. That chapter of your story was an important one, and it can't be ripped out. But you can write a new one.

Yes, people can get hurt. Yes, we can feel like we've wasted a lot of time. Yes, we can get mad at ourselves because we knew better. But here's the truth, and my point: *Connections are meant to be played out.* All of them. This is a part of life. We collide with people. We make decisions based on how we feel. Then we realize that other things were happening below the surface. We tried our best. It didn't work out. We can beat ourselves up for choices we now regret, wish they never happened, let those collisions become stains on our story, and then internalize and believe we are less than, defective, unlovable.

Or we can believe we needed to play it out.

The rock needed to be turned over, even if there was nothing there. Because discovering there was nothing there had value. Otherwise, we would have lived in regret. There was value in learning about ourselves and love through the process. This is the path that leads to acceptance and self-forgiveness. This is the path that leads to our evolution and learning about ourselves through love, especially lost love. It's not about why the relationship didn't work (going backward on the path) but rather what we were meant to learn from the collision (going forward on the path). Most of us get stuck in reverse. We dwell on "the one that got away," on what could have been, and stay locked in that gear. We shift gears when we start to believe (feel) we were meant to collide with the one we collided with. Because there is learning to be had from every collision—but only if we play it out.

Reminder

You needed to go through what you went through to know what you know now. Not all love is supposed to be forever. Each expired relationship is meant to connect you more to you.

The Blindsided Breakup

*Sometimes you have to get knocked down lower than
you've ever been to stand taller than you ever were.*
—ANONYMOUS

SPENCER AND LUV

Spencer called the suicide hotline—twice.

Although he had never gotten along with his mom, and
everyone knew that, he shared a special kind of closeness
with her that no one could truly understand. Well, unless
you also were raised by a young, single, codependent mom
with no tools who wasn't ready for a "difficult" son. What
formed between them was a sticky kind of dysfunctional
relationship bond that led to Al-Anon meetings for Spencer
as an adult.

Even with two years of therapy after his mom died, Spencer was still struggling to get up in the mornings. Which
is why our sessions were over FaceTime, my least favorite

way to see clients. I prefer coffee shops or a walk-and-talk around the lake here in Silverlake, California. Telehealth is legitimate now, the standard, but when I started my practice it was controversial and forbidden. It was why critics called me unconventional. It was also why I called myself a coach instead of a therapist. Therapists weren't supposed to see clients online. They also weren't supposed to post their own feelings and struggles as they went through a divorce and started over in life.

Okay, okay, the truth was, I wasn't just ahead of my time. I was broke. I couldn't afford an office. That's why I met my clients in coffee shops and at the lake.

Anyway, none of Spencer's friends understood why he took his mom's death so hard, except Luv Thomas. That's her real name. Her parents were hippies. Also alcoholics. She could relate to feeling alone. The big loss in her life was Fred the hamster when she was eleven. But who's to judge the depth of any relationship? Hamster or human, it doesn't matter. She knew what Spencer was going through.

Although Luv lived in another state, she was there for him. Like any good friend. Phone, FaceTime, daily texts. And he was there for her as she went through a loss of her own. A breakup with her "college sweetheart" of four years. He wasn't that sweet actually. He had been cheating on her for most of their relationship.

Two friends grieving a major loss in their lives combined with nosebleed tickets to a Pink concert and it was bound to happen.

After they kissed, things moved pretty quickly. The trust

and friendship tracks were already laid since they'd been "buds" forever. The train was already moving. They just needed to jump on, which they did. For Spencer, it was actually a plane. He moved to San Francisco, where he would work remotely and they could try to do what Harry and Sally couldn't.

It was an easy relationship. They rarely fought. He was good to her and made her feel seen, something she hadn't felt in a very long time. And she was the textbook good girlfriend. Supportive, caring. They had sex two times a week without fail. It helped that she made calendar invites.

This was all before she created and sold her start-up, a beauty line, back when she was a blogger. She recalled her first exhibit at a wellness convention, where she felt insecure and embarrassed, thinking no one would buy her candle holders that made inspirational quotes literally glow. She wanted to pack up and leave before the event even started, but Spencer stopped her, encouraging her to stay and give her products a chance. He grabbed her collection and started selling on the floor. When Spencer, a true introvert, stepped out of his comfort zone to do that, Luv realized how lucky she was. He was the first person in her life who believed in her.

So then why did she end it abruptly, with no warning, after three and a half years? There was no infidelity. No "let's work on this." No couples counseling. They were about to get a hamster, the first step toward "let's really do this."

Luv didn't have an explanation. At least not for Spencer. Because she didn't want to hurt him. But she told her therapist—spoiler, also me. She told me she knew exactly why she broke up with him. Or at least she thought she did. We all think we know until we dig deeper and realize what's really going on (more on this crucial point later).

Technically I wasn't seeing them as a couple. Generally speaking, you're not supposed to see clients as a couple if you are seeing them individually. The couple is one unit. But they weren't a couple when I was seeing them individually. I was seeing Spencer for help with the sudden death of his mother, and he referred his "acquaintance," Luv Thomas, to me for her "abandonment issues." Two months into seeing them as individual clients, they went to the Pink concert and the roller-coaster started.

Now they were talking to me about their issues with each other instead of about what each had originally come to see me for. This happens often in therapy. It's like taking your car in for an oil change and finding out that five thousand other pressing things need to be fixed. So I had to refer one of them out. Spencer thought Luv needed it more. (She did.) But not for the reason Spencer thought. What he didn't know was that she had no interest in fixing the relationship.

"I can't do this anymore," Luv confessed one morning in therapy. Before I could respond, she held up a shiny men's Rolex.

"What's that?" I asked.

"He slipped it in my bag."

"Who?"

"This guy. I didn't even get his name. We were sitting next to each other on the plane. Okay, we were flirting. We had crazy sexual chemistry. It's not like I was going to do anything. He went into the restroom and told me to follow him. But I didn't. I swear."

She was defeated and done. "I was never attracted to Spencer. There, I said it. It was a comfort thing. A timing thing. A safety thing."

As a therapist, you're supposed to meet your client where they're at. You're not supposed to sway them in their decisions but instead to fully accept their decisions. Not influence or control them. But I was so disappointed. I had spent the last six months helping her and Spencer work through their issues independently so they could build a healthy, sustainable relationship. I was invested in this too. I was rooting for them. And now she was done? Just like that? After experiencing "chemistry" on a plane?

"We're attracted to people all the time. It doesn't mean you should end your relationship."

"I've been in toxic relationships my entire life. Spencer represented healthy. He was what was *prescribed*, and I needed to take my medicine."

Luv broke up with Spencer that weekend. Over text. Spencer was completely blindsided. He was looking at engagement rings. And he didn't just lose his girlfriend. He lost his best friend—actually his only friend. Once they got together, he slowly lost his friends and made no effort to make new ones, since he was moving. And no, technically he didn't pack up and move his life for her—he'd always wanted to live on the West Coast and even had *Baywatch* posters over his bed—but he *kinda* did. He was thinking palm trees (Los Angeles), not bridges (San Francisco).

His first response to her when she broke up with him was "I'll work out more." He knew she liked abs. They once got into an argument after watching *Fight Club*. Luv convinced Spencer that some women are obsessed with abs. Just like men are obsessed with asses. But she assured him it wasn't his dad bod. He didn't understand. Why did she want out? She said what everyone says when they're afraid of confrontation: "You deserve better." And he did. But at the very least, he also deserved an in-person conversation.

She had already moved out of their apartment while he was out of town for his cousin's wedding. We could easily assume that the catalyst for the breakup was the sale of her start-up. Seven figures on the way to their bank can get anyone to make major life changes. *But she's not like that*, Spencer thought. Bullshit. Success is a real force, and it can rock any relationship. The guy on the plane—that wasn't just about sexual chemistry. He was a business broker, someone who sold companies like hers for a living. I've seen it happen many times. When opportunities you never thought you had or could have collide with your growing belief in your self-worth, the dynamics and feelings of your relationship can be directly affected. In Spencer and Luv's case, it magnified what was already there. Or not there. Magnets can flip pretty fast.

Success doesn't make people shitty. It makes people real. But professional momentum wasn't the sole reason Luv left:

She had also realized that safe and healthy wasn't enough anymore. Especially now. Spencer was totally in the dark, and she felt guilty about that. But breaking up with him was her truth. And if we don't start with truth, there will be no growth or understanding of self.

WHAT REALLY HAPPENED
"Blindsided" Just Means No One Was Talking

Blindsided breakups appear out of nowhere. You're confused, stunned, shocked, and genuinely don't see them coming. Things seemed good until you came home to an empty apartment. Zero warning. Just a note on the table or a text in your phone. But the truth is, you weren't blindsided. You just weren't informed of the other person's inner journey. Or you were, but you weren't listening.

My ex-wife may have had trouble expressing her feelings, but she did drop many hints that she was not happy in the marriage. I just brushed them off, minimizing what they meant. When one day she told me she wanted a separation, I felt blindsided. It *seemed* to come out of nowhere. The truth, though, is that I chose not to see what was brewing, the drift and the disconnect. On a deeper level, maybe I didn't want to face it. Because then I would have had to face myself.

Luv kept Spencer in the dark for most of the three years they were together. She was there, but she wasn't. She'd needed to feel safe while she rebuilt her self-worth after her previous history of abusive relationships. And the scheduled sex was more for her than for him—it proved she was a good girlfriend. Another box checked. The whole relationship was about worth for her—about rebuilding what others had taken from her in the past. Spencer was a stepping-stone.

Of course, this truth had been the undercurrent of the entire relationship, but she didn't understand it fully until she broke things off. It took a stranger on a plane for it to click. She was worth at least $15,000. She had proof—his Rolex. Sometimes a small gesture is all it takes to reveal our deep truths. It doesn't happen only after months of process-ing with your therapist. Although Luv knew for years that it wouldn't last with Spencer, she knew in just a moment that it was time to end it.

She blindsided Spencer because she didn't have the tools to express how she really felt, let alone tools to terminate a relationship. Many of us don't have the tools. We were raised in unsafe spaces where self-expression wasn't allowed or promoted. We stuffed things down and that became our go-to, our standard operating instructions. Then we grew up and struggled with expressing how we felt in adult rela-tionships because we didn't put in the reps to exercise that muscle.

If you were blindsided by a breakup, your ex probably didn't have the tools to do it any other way. It's not that they were a monster. Most likely, they didn't express themselves in the relationship and didn't know how to end it. I tried to get Luv to think about the tools she needed to develop.

"Luv, you can't just disappear without ending the rela-tionship. Spencer has huge abandonment issues. You know this."

Luv pulled out a box of licorice and stuck two in her mouth. When she was thinking, she had to eat. We had processed this and come to the conclusion that it wasn't a bad or unhealthy thing—she wasn't eating her feelings. It was like a walking and talking thing.

Then I reminded her, "Also, this is a great opportunity for you to not run. Instead, face your fears and have the hard conversation. This is your dragon, Luv. You have to slay it."

Like most of my clients, she didn't listen to me. She had a friend come over to help her pack and she cleared out all her stuff over the weekend. Left the place like she had never lived there. Luv didn't share any of this with me. She skipped a few sessions and didn't respond to my check-in emails. I only found out when Spencer contacted me for an "emergency session."

"I'm sorry she did this to you," I expressed sincerely.

"I don't know what to do. I've never lived alone before," Spencer confessed.

"Maybe it had to happen this way. Or it wouldn't have happened at all."

"She told me it wasn't me. She says she's been drifting for a while now. Did you know this? Do you know if there's someone else?"

"You know I can't tell you what we discuss in our sessions. But I will say that she has been working hard on self-expression and talking about her feelings."

He didn't hear anything I said. He wasn't in a place to listen. The proof was in what he said next.

"I moved here for her. What the fuck am I going to do now?"

I had no answers for him.

Safety as a Stepping-Stone

When we have been in abusive or toxic relationships, we continue to gravitate toward unhealthy dynamics unless we break the pattern and actively make a different choice. But sometimes we only choose safety. Then, once we feel safe, we realize this person is not for us. There is no chemistry. The relationship is a stepping-stone. A temporary safe haven.

Luv wasn't attracted to Spencer, only to the idea of him. He represented what was prescribed—healthy, calm, no surprises. He was the medicine she needed to take in order to heal from past abusive relationships. She didn't intentionally use him. Instead, she convinced herself that the attraction, the chemistry, would kick in later. That it was secondary and would grow over time.

Have you been in a relationship that made you feel like a stepping-stone? Have you had a partner who needed you at that time in their life but then "outgrew" you? Making you feel used and discarded? Maybe you internalized those feelings and wondered if the breakup happened because of you. Not so much because of what you did but because of who you are. A reaction like this can be very damaging, and it's very common. People can feel blindsided by the ending of these relationships because such endings are a reaction, not a response (more on this below).

We all have wounded, unhealed parts of ourselves. And as much work as we have done on ourselves, they still show up if we are not aware. Or when we make impulsive decisions. Luv's wounded self, the part of her that wasn't healed from previous abusive relationships, had her jumping from one bad relationship to another and not wanting to be in a healthy relationship. Healthy was strange and unfamiliar. Chaos was homeostasis. Her wounded self was used to chaos, not calm. She needed Spencer to be reactive, to throw a chair or break something, to react in a way that felt familiar. For her, chemistry was fueled by chaos.

Breaking up with Spencer was a reaction from Luv's wounded self—a reaction only compounded by her success in selling her company and the new attention she was receiving from other men. She didn't stay in it and work on building chemistry with Spencer by giving her body the experience of a new normal.

I often say that we must swim past the breakers to see what is truly there and figure out if anything can be built from that. It's important to know what's beyond the breakers because, if you realize the blindsiding was a reaction from a wound, it is much easier to create distance and internalize that being blindsided was not your fault or your own personal failure. Rather, it came from another person's refusal to sit with the uncomfortable to see what was on the other side.

Was there any guarantee that by staying and working on the relationship, chemistry and attraction would have flourished as Luv gave her body (not her mind) a new experience of love and attraction? Of course not. There is no guarantee with love. But chances are that a breakup would have been a conscious uncoupling (a response) rather than a blindsided breakup (a reaction).

The Truth Lives Under the Surface

They say there are three sides to every story: your side, their side, and the truth. Most only know their own side. When we play back our relationships, our memories and perceptions are subjective and can be influenced by various factors such as emotions, biases, and personal interpretations. Memory is not a perfect recording of past events. Colored by our current mindset and emotions, our recollections can be distorted and our understanding full of gaps. We tell the story we want to hear based on our own story and how we're wired, and so we consciously or unconsciously choose to amplify or minimize certain events.

A good example is people in abusive relationships. Have you been friends with someone who was in an abusive relationship? What did they usually do? They minimized the abusive episodes and highlighted the good times. Like anyone else, they remembered certain events more vividly while forgetting or downplaying others. This is why our exes often have very different recollections or interpretations of what happened in our relationship.

But here is the more important point. There is what happened on the surface—he cheated, she drifted, they gave up, she stayed even though she didn't want to—and there is what was really happening underneath: the *why*, the *driving force*, the *TRUTH*. This is the key that unlocks the understanding needed to get closure and finally break through. It's the heart ointment needed to heal. Otherwise, we're just peeling scabs. Without understanding what was happening underneath, we are left with twisted stories that lead to confusion, anger, and resentment. These stories also give us room to internalize what happened—by blaming ourselves, feeling we are less than or defective because the relationship didn't work, believing it was our fault.

Sometimes it was. But even if this was the case, if we know where our feelings and behavior come from—what's happening underneath—we have more compassion and understanding and we're better able to let go and break through.

On the surface: → He cheated.
What's happening underneath: → Low self-esteem and a constant need to be desired led him to act out.

On the surface: → She drifted.
What's happening underneath: → When they moved in together, her fear of intimacy caused her to love from a distance and emotionally check out.

On the surface: → He gave up.
What's happening underneath: → His deep core belief that he's not lovable (developed from his childhood) caused him to stop trying when things get hard.

On the surface: → She stayed in it even though she didn't love her or want to be in the relationship.

What's happening underneath: → Her fear of abandonment kept her in relationships she doesn't want to be in.

On the Other Side

When you're going through a blindsided breakup, you usually don't get to see what's happening inside the person who blindsided you. There is no communication or explanation. It's a hit-and-run. Not knowing why is what makes this type of breakup so difficult. This is when we start making up reasons that are not true. This is when we personalize, internalize, and shine a cruel black light on our own worth.

To help you see that your breakup probably had nothing to do with you, here's a snippet from a session with Luv in which I commented on what I believed she was truly saying.

"He deserves better than me," Luv announces. (Her wounded self didn't want to do the work, so Luv was taking an easy way out here.)

"Anyway, I've grown so much. Thanks to you. And it's not fair to be in something that doesn't feel honest. Right?" (If she could get me to agree with her action, then she didn't have to hold the guilt.)

"Yes," I agree, "you have grown. But you guys haven't done any work together as a couple. You guys haven't grown together, which can change the dynamic of the relationship. You do not share your inner journey with Spencer." (I was trying to get her to see that just working on herself wouldn't fix the problem and was only one piece of this.)

"I just finally feel like I deserve everything I've ever

dreamed of," Luv says. "I feel like I'm worth more than a dad bod." (Luv was using the term "dad bod" instead of speaking her truth—that selling her company had given her financial freedom, attention, and more opportunities.)

"This isn't about a dad bod, Luv. And you know it." (My invitation to her to go deeper.)

Luv glances at her phone. "Shit, I gotta go. But I'll see you next week. Great sesh." (Running away. Again.)

She looks me in the eye, sincerely. "Thank you," she says gently, under her breath. (Her way of saying goodbye because she knew this was her last session.)

Even though there were a dozen sessions that had led to that "thank you," I felt like we were just getting started. But that was the last time I ever saw Luv Thomas. And she just did to me what she did to Spencer, ended the relationship without warning—blindsided.

We believe that people blindside us because they are cowards. Because they're afraid to hurt us so they take the easy way out. That they stuff feelings down until it's too late and the relationship is no longer fixable. So they go off without warning.

Yes, blindsiding can feel like an act of violence. It's traumatic and damaging. But if you see it as a reaction to the refusal to work on self, you'll see that your partner is no monster but actually a wounded human. If blindsiding is kneejerk behavior based in not wanting to go deeper and truly examine self, false beliefs, and fears, then there is room for compassion and understanding—the vines that will pull you out of the quicksand.

Judging your partner's behavior is the fastest way to stop your own healing. You become angry and consumed by the belief that you're a victim. This is the most powerless state. It will keep your shoulders tense and your knuckles white. To break through, you must choose to understand the whole person and not just what they did but also what may have been happening internally for them.

As I mentioned, I have been blindsided (when I was married). But I have also blindsided. I left a three-year relationship only weeks after we admitted we were drifting and things didn't feel the same. But instead of working on the relationship and exploring what was going on within myself, I found a new apartment on Craigslist and used the excuse of not wanting to lose out on "a great deal in a prime location" as a way to exit as quickly as I could. I convinced myself that this was a fair move because she didn't stop me. She let me leave.

But the truth was that I didn't want to look at myself or my pattern of leaving relationships right around the three-year mark. It was my refusal to examine self that drove me to react—to leave fast, without warning or a conversation. In looking back, I see that it wasn't that she let me leave. Because of her wiring, she froze. She was in shock. She'd had an extremely traumatic childhood, with no one to protect her from her mentally unstable mom. She didn't say anything when I left because she'd gone into a survival state, not because she didn't want to work on the relationship.

BREAK-THROUGH WORK

A blindsided breakup can make the train jump the tracks. Your body may still be in a panic state. Your mind is still processing what happened. It's important that you ground yourself, get the train back on the tracks again, and reconnect to your body.

After a blindsided breakup, you need to prioritize your nervous system. Forget about everything else for now. Don't dissect the relationship or try to figure out what happened. You will want answers, an explanation. And the likelihood that they will not come will make you spin out of your body and into your head while your body is still in survival mode, stuck in fight-flight-or-freeze. Before you can start healing, your body needs to thaw out for everything to get back online again.

Your nervous system is what you should tag as priority number one and move way up to the top. As you're going about your day or week, check in with your nervous system constantly. (I literally place my hand on my heart and ask it what it needs.) Notice when you feel dysregulated. Do you feel panic and anxiety? Where is it coming from? What are you thinking about? What are you doing? Who's around you? What's activating the dysregulation? These are questions we typically don't ask ourselves. We either white-knuckle through our feelings or allow both our thoughts and our feelings to hijack us.

Take a few deep grounding breaths as you notice the feelings that come up. The anger. Hurt. Betrayal. Longing. Confusion. Know that what's being activated is your inner child, your younger self. A scab has been ripped from an old wound. You're not just feeling pain, sadness, and anger over the relationship. You're feeling abandoned like you did when your dad left. Or rejected like that time in summer camp when you were humiliated in front of your friends. Or you're validating a false belief, like "I'm not lovable," or "I'm not good enough," or "I don't deserve healthy love."

There is always something else running under our feelings, and tapping into that truth is what will help you understand and create the distance that enables healing to take place. This is the break-through work. What does this work look like? It's what we work on in therapy rooms, exploring what activates us by connecting dots from what we feel now to what we have gone through, because everything is tied to our story. If we don't do this work—if we don't look deeper and go on an inner explorative journey—we will go through the motions of the breakup on the outside while on the inside we may be hardening our hearts and amplifying our fears and false beliefs about ourselves. This leaves us loving soft. Loving from a distance. Loving with fists instead of open palms. And setting ourselves up for the same relationship experiences in the future, the same results, and the same lack of growth.

Love Yourself the Way Your Parents Could Not

Our parents didn't give most of us the emotional milk we needed to develop healthy sense-of-self bones. They might have fed us and bought us designer jeans. But they didn't create a space for us to express our inner journey. They didn't encourage feelings or set an example of what expressing yourself and your needs looked like. They may have warned us about strangers and drugs but failed to teach us how to draw boundaries to protect our inner self. Their focus on what we did rather than who we were made us tie our worth to our accomplishments. So when we became adults, we did a lot of things but were disconnected from ourselves. We got busy loving other people but not ourselves. We didn't know what loving ourselves looked like. We'd never had a chance to practice it. We were never taught.

To reparent ourselves is to nurture and care for ourselves in ways we may not have experienced as a child. This is a foundational piece in our healing journey. Not nurturing and caring for ourselves (because most of us don't know how, especially men) contributes to the drift, conflict, reactions, unhealthy patterns, internalization, and eventually expiration that show up in all our relationships.

After a breakup is the perfect time to take a beat and start this practice. The canvas is clean, and you can start fresh by first creating a new relationship with yourself. Doing this is a gift to yourself of a corrective love experience. Not from someone else. From you. You are taking the power back and reconditioning your body, mind, heart, and soul, restoring their worth. This process connects you back to self and an authentic sense of value that is earned, not given to you by someone else. It ignites your becoming.

If you don't actively practice loving yourself the way you should have been loved as a child, rewiring and reconditioning your body, you will remain in a state of dysregulation caused by past traumas. You'll stay locked in survival mode, the way you grew up. You'll still be a walking reaction, loving as a wounded child instead of an evolving adult. And most likely, you will recycle relationships, experiencing the same kind of love over and over, just with different people. Reparenting yourself will break that cycle. Because, as you change, what you are drawn to and want for yourself will change.

Here's how to start reparenting yourself after a blindsided breakup.

Self-Compassion

A blindsided breakup, more than other kinds, can make you hard on yourself. *I should have known. I should have seen it coming,* you tell yourself. It is so important to be gentle with yourself, especially while the breakup is fresh. You may not yet be in a place to roll up your sleeves and do the work of sitting in therapy rooms to rebuild and redesign your life. You may barely be able to get out of bed and make yourself a cup of coffee. If so, it's okay. Be kind to yourself. Be patient. Give yourself what you need. And if that's sending callers to voicemail and unplugging for a couple of weeks, good, go ahead. Feel what you need to feel. Go through what you need to go through.

But you do need to be honest with yourself. You do have to know when you are giving yourself healthy space and when you're just hiding. Reparenting is also about picking yourself back up and moving forward and through, even during the hard days. Healthy parents gave us discipline and structure and a needed push. You must be able to give that to yourself now.

Identify Your Needs

Most of us struggle with giving ourselves what we need. We're great at fulfilling other people's needs, but not our own. Before we can give ourselves what we need, though, we need to know what our needs are. We have not paid attention to ourselves in that way. *What do I truly need? Is it a need or an extra? Is it realistic? Is it arrogant of me? Am I making it all about me?* We may know what we need to build a better body or to meet financial or career goals. But reparenting ourselves means fulfilling our emotional needs. Do you need praise, validation, reassurance, admiration? Do you need to feel special, appreciated, valued, understood, wanted, seen, heard, safe, loved? Can you satisfy your own needs instead of depending on others to do that? Do you need to set new boundaries? Do you need a safe space for expressing yourself? How are you fulfilling your creative, sexual, and spiritual needs?

Inner Dialogue: Releasing Blame

Most of us don't talk to ourselves like we do to the people we love. We are not only hard on ourselves, but abusive. We assassinate our character. We belittle and blame ourselves constantly. Imagine the damage you would do to friendships if you spoke to your friends the way you speak to yourself. (Hint: you wouldn't have any.) Our negative dialogue with self is an unhealthy habit from childhood that began when we didn't meet the expectations of our parents. So we turned inward and blamed ourselves. The behavior associated with the self-hatred generated by this blame was talking to ourselves harshly. And since no one can hear it, we get away with talking to ourselves this way for years. An important step in reparenting is changing the way we speak to ourselves, to start talking to ourselves as we would our child or our grandparents. With love and kindness. With patience and warmth. With respect and understanding.

Healthy Boundaries

I mentioned boundaries as one of our needs, but I want to go deeper and wider here on establishing healthy boundaries, since it's such an integral part of reparenting ourselves. From childhood, we're often taught to bend and mold ourselves to make others comfortable. So we find it difficult to set appropriate boundaries as we get older. We don't know how. We have not put in the reps. We don't want to hurt or offend others, even at the risk of hurting ourselves—and our relationship with self. The violation of our personal space can cause us to break up with ourselves. Here are some types of boundaries that you may need to affirm or redraw for yourself:

Physical contact—You may not feel comfortable, for example, hugging someone you just met.

Verbal interactions—You may find it hard to accept when friends and family members speak to you in ways you don't like.

Personal space—You may choose not to have people in your personal space when you don't want them there. Any personal space that is yours can be your creative space or your reset space.

Other types of boundaries protect your well-being more generally:

Emotional—Protecting your emotional state

Physical—Protecting your physical space

Sexual—Protecting your sexual needs and safety

Workplace—Not allowing your work to be your life and protecting yourself from anything toxic at work

Material—Protecting what belongs to you

Time—Protecting the use of your time and preventing its misuse

What new boundaries do you need to draw to start re-parenting yourself?

Emotional Regulation—"Body Consciousness"

Most of us have not acquired the tools to manage and regulate our emotions and to find healthy outlets for them. Instead, we stuff down feelings, go numb, or explode in angry outbursts. We eat and run toward our addictions to avoid feeling. To reparent ourselves, we must learn how to regulate our emotions. The way in is through our bodies, not our minds. When we feel dysregulated, our thoughts mirror that. If your body is dysregulated, your thoughts are distressful and spinning, you feel out of control, and you are certain that everything is *not* going to be okay, causing more anxiety and dysregulation. So you want to turn away from your thoughts and move into your body.

In the belief that emotional regulation is a thinking process, many people try to think through their emotions instead of feeling through them, not understanding that it's a process of dropping into their bodies. Practice noticing how your emotions manifest in your body. The tension in your shoulders. The turning of your gut. The tightening of your neck. (I bite my lips.) Don't label or judge these manifestations. Just notice them. This is body consciousness— being attuned to and mindful of the physical sensations, movements, and experiences within your body (including your heart). Once you connect with your body's signals and how emotions manifest physically, you can regulate those emotions by exploring and understanding where they're coming from. In other words, it's not just about allowing yourself to feel and knowing how feelings manifest in your body, but also about exploring and understanding what's activating your feelings. When you understand the origin of how feelings manifest in your body, you no longer think of your body as a monster, as you've done since the first time it felt this way. Instead, you experience real feelings from real stories that flow through you instead of getting clogged, keeping your emotions dysregulated and you reactive.

Anchors: Positive Reinforcement Spaces

In my first book, I talk about "life containers" and the power of the safe spaces we create for ourselves. Like a greenhouse, these spaces promote our growth instead of stunting it. After a blindsided breakup, it's important to create "anchors"—positive reinforcement spaces in your life—and to be protective of them and intentional about them so they can give you continuous structure, calm, and a new homeostasis.

Anchors can be anything from your circle of friends to a daily ice plunge. Anchors are any spaces that help ground you and stabilize your nervous system. They are your "safe tree" where your body can be convinced that you are protecting it and that it's safe. Anchors promote play and flow states and should be threaded into your daily life. They are not spaces you visit but spaces that are baked into your day-to-day. Here are some of mine:

A mindfulness walk or hike
A motorcycle ride (doesn't have to be long—twenty
   minutes to the gym works wonders)
Nature
Daily ice plunges (preferably three minutes each)
Writing and creative space
Meals and meaningful conversations with friends

Sauna (thirty minutes each, three times a week)

A CrossFit workout

Being intentional and mindful of the positive reinforcement spaces in your life will not only help ground you but also get you out of your head and its spinning thoughts. In your head is the most dangerous place to be after a blindsided breakup.

Tip: Have Smart Feet

Having "smart feet" got me through some of the hardest days of my divorce. What does it mean to have smart feet? It means trusting that your feet will take you somewhere and that when you get there things will fall into place. The engine will turn. You will stop ruminating. Just focus on getting to that space.

My smart feet usually took me to the gym. I put all my energy into just getting my ass to a class. Even if I didn't want to—*especially* if I didn't want to. I just told myself I needed to have smart feet and then I got there. Before thinking, before fear and ambivalence set in like tear gas, I just got moving. Once I got to class, the structure of the class forced me not only to sweat but also to engage with others, and being social kept me from drowning in feelings and my own problems. It got me out of my house and out of my head.

Getting out of my head was key. I used the community at the gym not just to make myself accountable but also to hear other people's stories and what they were going through. It reminded me that there are other people in this world, going through their own shit. Or living amazing lives. I told myself to notice them. Their eye colors. Their smiles. The warmth of their hugs.

I didn't know this at the time, but I was using mindfulness to stop the spinning thoughts in my head. Letting smart feet take me to a positive reinforcement space pulled me out of what was and back to living in what is. Even if only for an hour. Because an hour a day becomes seven hours a week. And the gym was just one of those spaces. I also had smart feet when it came to meeting up with friends. Or getting to a diner where I would journal, listen to an audiobook, buy myself a nice meal, and get comfortable being with me.

Where would your smart feet take you?

It doesn't have to be a gym. It could be a yoga class. A hike. Maybe the beach so you can feel sand between your toes and wind on your face. Maybe smart feet get you to poker night or the weekly Monday night dinner with your friends, which you actually don't even enjoy sometimes. Maybe a CODA meeting. A group bike ride. Or a writing class, because you finally have time to finish your book.

Let smart feet take you to whatever will help you get out of your house and out of your head. That's all that matters. Out of your house. Out of your house. As. Much. As. You. Can.

Another Tip: Take Notice

What does noticing look like for you? Set the intention to use all your senses, which will drop you into life and keep you out of your head. Imagine you are an alien who has come to this planet for the first time. Everything is new. What would you notice? What would you be curious about? What details would you pay attention to? How would you approach people? With this mindset, can you go into the same experiences you've had in the past, but with new lenses that will make them new?

Reminder

How someone decides to leave a relationship says more about that person and where they're at in their life than it does about you or the relationship.

The Flat Soda Breakup

"We Should Have Broken Up Years Ago"

There is an ocean of silence between us . . .
and I feel like I'm drowning in it.

—ANONYMOUS

OLIVIA AND KEN

It wasn't her dad's emotional neglect that caused her to chase older men. It wasn't her mom's inconsistent love that led to a fear of abandonment, a need for excessive reassurance, and constant anxiety about the stability of her intimate relationships. Olivia worked through all this in her twenties and early thirties. She was finally at a great place in her life. She was no longer a workaholic. She had built a solid PR company that ran itself, giving her time to finally live her life and find joy in the little things. She also had the "perfect" man. Her friends called him Ken, even though his real name was Kevin.

Ken also had his shit together. He was in therapy, had his own friends and hobbies. He took care of himself, physically, mentally, and emotionally. He bought candles but also did Iron Mans. He was a man's man and a woman's man. He understood things like "mental load" and had a true desire to be a great dad one day. He even went to see the Barbie movie—by himself.

When Olivia and Ken came to see me, I was a bit confused at first. There was no existing problem, nothing to diagnose. Then Olivia confessed that she had heard me say on one of my podcasts, "When clients tell me they never fight, it's a red flag." They wanted a confirmation that they were okay, a professional seal of approval before they got married.

Olivia and Ken had passed the three-year make-or-break mark two years earlier and had now gone to the next level— engaged and living together with a dog in a beautiful apartment in Brooklyn. There was no turbulence in their lives. They communicated well. Had sex twice a week. Shared common values and life goals. There was no underlying anger or resentment. They really seemed like a solid couple. Then I noticed something. Every time Olivia talked about their wedding or future, she would play with her engagement ring. When I asked her about it, she told me she hadn't even noticed.

"I don't understand. Why is that a thing?" she asked, slightly defensive.

"It may not be anything. I just noticed," I said matter-of-factly.

"I think she's nervous about the wedding," Ken interjected.

"Are *you* nervous about the wedding?" I asked Ken. I sensed some projection.

There was a slight pause.

"I mean, we're spending a lot of money on it," he said.

I noticed Olivia was now turning her ring in circles.

"Do you guys want to get married?" I asked.

They looked at each other first. Then—"Of course we do," Olivia said.

"What kind of question is that?" Ken asked.

It was a question to see whether each of them answered it on their own or whether they looked at each other for approval—to see what the other was thinking. It was almost like they were subconsciously playing chicken. This was when I knew their relationship wasn't perfect. Nothing was wrong, but nothing wrong doesn't always mean nothing's wrong.

Their relationship was on cruise control. It was flat soda. They were going through the motions of what a couple should do after five years of being together. Tying the knot. Buying a house. Having kids. But I felt like they didn't want all that and I didn't know why. The problem was that they didn't know either. So I bookmarked the moment and changed the subject.

After that session, Olivia and Ken started coming in late and even canceled a few times. They weren't as consistent as they'd been when they first started therapy. I knew what was happening: their relationship was a ticking clock. I knew because I see this pattern in so many of my clients who are afraid to admit they're in something that maybe they don't want. When Olivia and Ken finally came in for a session, I was more direct with my questions.

"I want each of you to tell me why you're in this. Just as an exercise. Don't overthink it. Don't try to protect each other. Just be completely honest."

I ask this question often as a temperature check. It catches clients off guard. But Olivia and Ken didn't look confused. They looked scared. "Well, he's good to me," she said. "We've been together for five years," Ken added. "We never fight," they both agreed.

Their answers were logical. But the temperature check wasn't just about how they answered this vulnerable question. I studied their body language. Seeing the engagement live in the room can be very telling. Olivia and Ken didn't even look at each other, and they kept their hands to themselves.

As we processed more and more of their feelings about each other and the relationship, they came to the realization that they weren't in love anymore. They were together because it made sense. They had built a good life together. They liked the same things. They had common friends. But they were more like friends with benefits than lovers.

They found all this extremely hard to admit. I could tell they didn't want to hurt each other's feelings. But once it came out, there were no hurt feelings because they were in agreement. There was only sadness. The passion had faded. The butterflies had flown away. They admitted that the sex was mechanical, and that both of them had been drifting. It had been like this for a long time, they confessed. Yes, love is a choice. But when the chemistry is gone and the relationship isn't what they want anymore, the choice to stay may be more damaging than the choice to leave. The soda wasn't just flat. They didn't want to drink it anymore.

Learning about the true state of their relationship made me emotional as well. I felt their sadness, the knowing that something they built and shared had grown for a while but now had died. I've been there myself. I too have been afraid to end something that I knew was already over.

This was when they held each other and began to sob uncontrollably. No anger. No resentment. Just pure acceptance and pain. Like having to put your dog down because you know it's time and you don't want it to suffer anymore. It was beautiful to see two people holding space for each other without blame or defense, which is what the room is usually filled with. They just sat there and cried.

WHAT REALLY HAPPENED

Olivia and Ken didn't break up after that session. They were logical, determined people with growth mindsets. They could fix this. But you can't fix feelings. They took tantra classes. They went on an exotic trip together. They even separated for a month, just to see if it would rekindle the original spark. It didn't. It actually confirmed what they were already feeling: irreversible secondary change. Their relationship had become platonic. Basically, they were friends with benefits, for years now. Finally they decided to end their relationship.

BREAK UP ON PURPOSE

Olivia and Ken handled their breakup very differently. They had wanted to "consciously uncouple." Because that's what healthy people who have "done the work" do. End the relationship with love and kindness and remain friends who are still in each other's life. Or at least, that was their intention, but their reactions to the breakup were very different.

Olivia got on the apps and started dating right away. She dated younger men who were the complete opposite of Ken. Men who lived in the moment, without plans or a 401(k). She wanted passion. Make-up sex. Breakfast in bed (Ken's pet peeve was crumbs in the bed). She didn't want someone who made sense. She was sick of checking off boxes. She'd been doing that since she was fourteen. She wanted to make decisions based on what she felt in the here and now, not on what was best for her future. So she went to concerts and woke up in studio apartments she would never have lived in. She rode on the back of motorcycles, which she had always been against, even when Ken wanted one.

Olivia got into a relationship pretty quickly, just two months after the breakup. His name was Rad, believe it or not. His full name was Radley but everyone called him Rad. His name alone would have been a deal breaker before, but Olivia was a different person now. Or had she been different for a while, but her relationship with Ken prevented her from showing her true growing self? Or was she now numbing, running away from self, acting out in a way? Only she would know.

Ken seemed to go the other way, but it was just his version of the same thing. He wasn't looking for love. He didn't get on the apps. Instead, he wanted adventure. He wanted to travel and "find himself." He bought a van and drove across the country, documenting his van life journey. He swam in rivers. Went on solo hikes. Made s'mores in the woods. And documented every moment for the world to see in real time. But Ken didn't process where he was at emotionally or reflect on his relationship with Olivia. He just filled his life with lots of activities and instructional videos on how to live an adventurous life. I have to admit, some very impressive shots of sunsets and sipping morning coffee in the woods from a vintage percolator made me want to experience his life on the road. There was great presentation there. But zero processing.

Sometimes people leave relationships and then do surprising things. We often see this on social media. A lawyer who was married for ten years gets divorced, quits her job, falls in love with a surfer, and becomes a meditation teacher in Costa Rica. Or two weeks after a breakup, she's under a tree in a park, wide-eyed and with hands over her mouth because the person she swiped on a week ago is down on one knee holding a ring.

There's nothing wrong with changing your entire life. I think it's a great thing. You should always pursue your truth and your passions. But only if you're running toward yourself and not away. Many people get into a new relationship too fast and drastically change their lives. Then the bottom falls out when reality hits and they see it was more of a distraction than healing and truth. They skipped the part about "Single. On Purpose." And their growth calcified.

What Olivia and Ken didn't do was grieve. They broke free before the recess bell rang. Actually, they ditched school. Yes, you shouldn't isolate at home and eat your feelings, but you do need to grieve, reflect, and give yourself space for revelations about self and love and why the plane went down. This understanding is how we close that chapter. Yes, you can be grieving while also climbing rocks and dating someone new (whenever you honestly feel ready to), but you must do it. You can't just pause that part of your inner life and then somehow skip ahead. You will have to un-pause and process your grief at some point.

If you don't allow yourself to grieve the loss of the relationship, you may feel okay as long as your calendar is filled with exciting trips and new dates, but eventually the dust will settle. And when it does, the feelings will hit. Hard. The more you distract and avoid the feelings, the higher the cliff you'll need to climb. Then when you fall, you really fall. It's the same when a parent or best friend passes away and you don't think about it much and move on with your life. Friends are surprised it hasn't affected you. "It's weird. Her dad died and she never cried." Then one day it hits and you fall into a depression because you never grieved your loss. You never gave your body what it needed to feel. Breakups are the same.

BREAK-THROUGH WORK

Sometimes a mutual breakup is more difficult to get through than any other type of breakup. It's easier to be angry at your ex. To point fingers and cast blame. To draw a line and say you don't want toxic and unhealthy anymore, you deserve someone who won't cheat on you. But with a mutual breakup, there are no other feelings like anger to distract you from the sadness. It's just pure loss, undisguised death. The only blame you place may be on yourself, for not ending it sooner.

But there is good news about a mutual understanding that a relationship has run its course and it's time to part, with no hard feelings but an acknowledgment that love has permanently changed. It hangs on what Resmaa Menaken calls "clean pain." Clean pain is what mends us and builds our capacity for growth. We say what needs saying, draw boundary lines that need drawing, and don't pass on our trauma to others. "Dirty pain" is the pain of avoidance, blame, or denial. Responding to situations from our most wounded parts is a major component in many breakups, and the reason why they can be so traumatic. Unlike a blindsided breakup, if your relationship has fizzled out and both of you have decided that the relationship has died and there's nothing more to do but go your own ways, the first step is to reframe what happened.

Reframing What Happened

A mental reframe is the process of consciously changing your perspective or mindset about a particular situation, thought, or belief by shifting how you think about it, interpret it, and attribute meaning to it. A mental reframe enables you to see it in a different light—to take a fresh new perspective. With a flat soda breakup, it helps prevent you from looking in the rearview and gives you a wide view of what's ahead—acceptance.

1. A study published in the *Journal of Personality and Social Psychology* found that individuals who engaged in positive reinterpretation (reframing) after a romantic breakup experienced better emotional well-being over time. These cognitive strategies included finding personal strengths, focusing on personal growth, and viewing the breakup as an opportunity for self-improvement.

2. Another study, published in the *Journal of Social and Personal Relationships*, explored the impact of cognitive reappraisal—a form of reframing—on emotional adjustment after a relationship breakup. The findings indicated that individuals who engaged in cognitive reappraisal experienced lower levels of distress and greater psychological well-being compared to those who used less adaptive coping strategies.

3. A research article published in the *Journal of Divorce and Remarriage* investigated the role of positive reframing in coping with divorce. The study found that individuals who engaged in positive reinterpretation and reframing of the divorce experience reported higher levels of post-divorce adjustment and life satisfaction.

Here's the reframe of a flat soda breakup, simple yet powerful:

YOUR RELATIONSHIP HAS EXPIRED.

I understand that this can sound minimizing. Hearts were involved. You both loved with everything you had. To say it simply expired feels disrespectful to what the two of you shared and tried to build. I get it. One can even argue that it's wrong. To be honest, I don't know if it's right or wrong to reframe your breakup as an expired relationship. That's not my focus. My focus is to give you tools, and this is an effective one.

The point of a reframe is to feel different about something by looking at it from a new angle. This shift in perspective produces a new feeling about it, encouraging insights and ultimately changes in behavior. This simple reframe has helped me and my clients tremendously. The word "breakup" invokes blame, shame, and panic and connotes something that fell apart, something that no longer exists. *What now? How do I fix it? What's going to happen to me and my life?* The word also opens the door to internalization. *Is there something wrong with me? Am I the reason it broke?* The word "breakup" makes it difficult to get to acceptance. And without acceptance or at least moving toward acceptance, you will be stuck and spinning. This is true of acceptance generally, not just with breakups.

No acceptance ➔ resistance ➔ suffering

Reframing your breakup as an expired relationship can help you accept what happened. The framing "My partner left me, broke up with me, and doesn't want to be with me" produces a very different feeling from "Our relationship has run its course. It was not meant to last a day longer or end a day sooner. It has expired." This reframing brings a calm that feels greater than you, making it easier to let go. There is no fight, only a release. A deep breath. A break between the acts in your story, not the concluding scene.

Reframing is also a practice. Stating your reframing out loud just once won't keep you from wondering what could have been. Use it more like a mantra. A reminder for when you're spinning. A mental realignment every time you get into your head and start playing back the highlight (or low-light) reel. *What if I'd been more . . .? What if they'd just been willing to . . . ?* What if, what if, what if. The what-ifs keep you holding on, stuck in the past—peeling scabs. The way you break free is through acceptance, radical acceptance. And the best way to accept what happened is to believe your relationship has expired.

Make it your daily mantra. Say it out loud. There is power in saying, repeatedly: *My relationship has expired. It was not meant to last one day more or less. It has run its course. We did the best we could with where we were at in our lives.*

Know That You Are Grieving

All breakups require going through a grieving process. Many involved in a mutual breakup don't believe it's necessary because the relationship may seem to have died a long time ago. Ending it can feel more like freedom than anything else. You *can* imagine life without your ex. You actually have been able to for a while now. It may *not* feel like the bottom fell out. There is no giant hole there. You may not feel empty and purposeless but rather full of hope and energy and excitement over creating a new life and all the possibilities that come with that.

That may all be true. But what's also true is that you just lost a significant part of your life. You lost a part of yourself. When a relationship dies, a part of us dies with it. And if you don't acknowledge that and allow yourself to grieve the death of the relationship and the parts of you that loved being in that relationship, the break won't be clean. There will be heart residue. All ruptures require repair. The tricky thing about a mutual breakup is that it may not feel like a rupture.

The Stages of Grief of an Expired Relationship

It's important to interpret the following stages of grief loosely. They come in no particular chronological order. You may loop back to a stage you've already experienced, or find yourself in two stages at the same time. What's important about knowing about the stages of grief is having a general guideline of what to expect. They normalize what you're going through, but remember: What you're going through is unique to your own expired relationship. It isn't like anyone else's, or like any of your previous expirations.

1. **Denial and Shock**

   At first there is numbed disbelief. You deny the reality of the breakup at some level in order to avoid the pain. *This isn't happening. It can't be. It's not.* The shock also provides emotional protection by preventing you from being over-whelmed all at once. When people ask if you guys are no longer together, you literally deny it. Because you're going to fix this. It's happening but it's not, because it's tempo-rary. *We're on hiatus, taking a break.* It's a misunderstand-ing. It's not over. It's a reset.

Examples of emotions during this stage of grief:

Mourning

Sadness

Confusion

Discomfort

2. Pain and Guilt

Now the feelings kick in. Hard. As the shock wears off, it is replaced with pain. Although excruciating and unbear-able at times, it is important that you experience the pain fully and not hide from it or try to avoid it or escape from it. You've heard the phrase "The only way out is through." In this case, "through" means allowing yourself to feel.

To me, this is the hardest stage. No one teaches us how to feel and how to be okay with our feelings. We run, hide, numb, and resist. Feelings are uncomfortable. Many will do anything to avoid feeling. This is where many of us turn to our vices. You are very vulnerable in this stage, so it's im-portant to ask for support if you don't trust what you'll do.

Painful feelings can be soul shattering. Nothing in life matters when you feel this way, and to sit and welcome them, to fully feel them, can feel like water torture. To allow the tears without judgment, labels, or solutions. To accept and just feel. This is extremely difficult, especially if you're someone who is not used to allowing yourself to feel in this way.

You may also have guilt, regret, and remorse over things you did or didn't do. How you showed up, or didn't show up. Over things that could have been avoided, preventing this suffering and pain.

Examples of emotions during this stage of pain and guilt:

Pain

Chaos

Loneliness

Fear

3. **Anger and Bargaining**

Now you're getting ready to stand back up. You've gotten up on one knee. And you're pissed. Furious. Angry at what happened. How things went down. What you sacrificed. Everything you suppressed is now surfacing like the villain in the basement making electric whips while Iron Man is glowing in his fame. Shit's about to go down.

Frustration gives way to anger, and you may lash out in various ways. Please try to process these feelings in a therapy room. Pouring sugar in gas tanks and trying to ruin your ex's life is wasted energy. Remember, this is a stage and these feelings will subside.

Some healthy things to do with your anger:

Fitness: Feel good in your body.

Travel: See more of the world.

Art: Express your feels visually.

Rock climbing, surfing, motorcycle riding, etc.: Pour your anger into a new hobby.

Write, journal, blog: Put it all down on paper. It's therapeutic. Help others with what you're going through.

You may also swing the other way and try to bargain during this stage to get your ex back. "I will go to therapy if you come back!" Chances are, you don't really want to revive the relationship, though you won't know that until later. Right now, your body is seeking homeostasis. Your lenses are not clear. You are reaching for a life raft, and that's what bargaining for a round two may look like. It's okay. It's normal. And it will pass. Sit with it. Do not react.

Examples of emotions during the anger and bargaining stage:

Anger

Resentment

Bargaining

Stubbornness

4. **Depression and Reflection**

While your friends think you should be getting on with your life and are already setting you up on blind dates, you may fall into sad reflection for a while. This is a normal stage of grief, so it's okay to not force yourself to meet new people and get on dating apps if that's not where you're at. The pressure you're getting from your friends to "get back out there" is more about them than about you. They just don't know it. They think they're being helpful. Communicate where you're at. Set boundaries, and express your needs and truth.

This is the stage where you realize the true magnitude of your loss. It depresses you, and that's okay. It doesn't mean you have fallen down a slippery well. It doesn't mean you have snapped back like a rubber band or that you're not moving forward. You may isolate yourself on purpose, reflect on things you did with your ex, and scroll through digital memories of the past. It's all okay. Don't judge it or label it. Like the pain stage, this is a time when you need to allow yourself to feel and reflect. Remember, the only way out is through, and you are going through.

Examples of emotions during the depression and reflection stage:

Depressed

Heavy

Crushed

Frustrated

Empty

Despairing

Now, what's *not* okay is staying in this state. Living there. Allowing yourself to feel depressed as you reflect and sit in the bathwater of your expired relationship is very different from wallowing, feeling sorry for yourself, and isolating for months. You don't have to wash your hair, eat greens, and go to the gym every day. But locking doors, sending friends to voicemail, and praying in front of a shrine you've built to your ex and/or expired relationship is not healing.

5. **Standing Up**

As you work through your feelings, reflecting (in a healthy way, which we'll get into later) and starting to adjust to life without your partner, the haze will clear. You'll go from a fetal position on the bathroom floor to up on one knee like a boxer believing in herself again. You will have more energy and calm. Your physical symptoms will lessen and your depressed state will begin to lift. There will be random moments when things hit again and you find yourself sobbing. For some reason, you'll discover, this usually happens when you're on the toilet.

But moments like this will occur less and less often. You'll stay in them less and less. You'll unlock your front door and smile at the Amazon guy again. Start to be more social and engage in life. And that light at the end of the tunnel will be shining next to friends with banners that say, HURRY THE FUCK UP! WE MISS YOU! And for the first time in a long time, you'll smile.

Examples of emotions during the standing-up stage:
Stronger
Motivated
Awakened
Hopeful

6. **Reconnection → Rebirth**

The dust has now settled. You can see both what's right in front of you *and* what's ahead—what you couldn't see before. It may be a tad blurry, but you can make things out. You may only be able to see your hand, but you're not in a deep ditch anymore. And with new lenses comes a new perspective and a new focus: You.

This is when you go back to the gym. Call friends back. All the ways I recommended earlier to channel your anger you're doing now without the anger. It's been replaced with joy and passion and self-worth. You are finally— maybe for the first time in your life—putting yourself first. It may feel strange at first. But keep pedaling that bike and it will start to feel empowering. You have turned that bib you were wearing in the denial stage completely around. It is now a cape.

Examples of emotions during the reconnection and rebirth stage:

Inspired

Determined

Refreshed

Empowered

7. Acceptance and Hope

Acceptance doesn't mean instant happiness. It just means you have swum too far to turn back and experienced secondary change—change that is not reversible. You have accepted what was. It may still hurt, but that gut-wrenching pain is gone. You can breathe. You notice breezes and feel the sun on your face again. Life is no longer on pause. You finally see hope, even if it's blurry and far away.

You have also accepted that the superhero feeling you experienced in the reconnection → rebirth stage is not sustainable. You have now evened out. Come back to earth.

You're still on the path to connection to self and a rebirth, but you're not seeing a therapist twice a week and reading three self-help books at once. You understand that you're running a marathon, not a sprint. You are calm, collected, grounded, and ready to enter by opening the door instead of kicking it down. Because you have nothing to prove anymore.

Examples of emotions during this stage of grief:

Hopeful

Comforted

Relaxed

Secure

Here are some things you don't have control over:

- Your ex's feelings
- Your ex's behavior
- What happened
- How the relationship ended
- How you could have loved
- How your ex or other people feel about you and the expired relationship
- Who your ex chooses to love next and when
- How your friends or your ex's friends choose to see what happened
- How your ex's friends behave toward you
- How long it will take you to grieve this relationship and rebuild

As I mentioned earlier, the seven stages of grief and loss for your expired relationship are not linear. This means you can feel like you've gotten as far as the standing-up stage, then snap back to anger and bargaining, then slide into denial before arriving at acceptance. It's different for everyone, and there are no timelines. You may stay in one stage for months and in another for two weeks. This is why healing is not a blanket but rather a custom-made quilt.

And no breakup is the same as another. Comparing what you're going through now with what you went through with the last one is not fair. Every breakup is different because every relationship is different. Also, who you were in your last expired relationship was different from who you are now and who you will be in the next one. There is no constant. No color-by-numbers. You are splattering paint until a picture emerges. Like a work of art, this breakup is one of a kind.

Journaling Prompt

Imagine that the expiration of your relationship is like the passing of a good friend or family member. Don't think about why they died, or whose fault it was for the relationship expiring. Focus on the feelings that would arise when a loved one dies. Write down how you would feel about this death. No labels or judgment. Just what you feel.

The purpose of this exercise is to allow yourself to feel. Anger, denial, jealousy, acceptance, whatever feelings come up. And if no feelings come up, what are you feeling about that? Again without blaming or judging, just put feelings down on paper as a practice and to give yourself permission.

Physical Changes

Grieving is a complex process. The emotional experience of loss induces both chemical and structural changes. The amygdala, responsible for processing emotions like fear and anxiety, becomes more active. This heightened activity can increase feelings of sadness, anxiety, and distress. The prefrontal cortex, which governs decision-making and regulation of emotions, can show reduced activity. This might lead to difficulties in making choices and managing emotional responses effectively, such as:

Neurotransmitter imbalances: You might experience imbalances in mood regulation and pleasure. Lower levels of serotonin are associated with feelings of depression, while changes in dopamine levels can affect motivation and reward.

Hormonal changes: The stress hormone cortisol can increase, affecting sleep patterns, appetite, and overall stress levels. Impacts on the hippocampus, responsible for memory processing, can include difficulty in recalling memories or details associated with the loss.

Endorphin release: Grieving individuals might experience physical and emotional discomfort from lower levels of endorphins, which are natural painkillers and mood enhancers.

Neural pathway rewiring: Over time, the brain might

rewire certain neural pathways to adapt to the loss. This can lead to changes in perception, priorities, and even personality.

Sleep disturbances: Grief can disrupt sleep patterns, changing overall brain function and emotional well-being.

Reminder

There is no time frame or blueprint when it comes to grieving. We all grieve in different ways. Every loss is different. What's important is that you start the process.

Your Breakup Is Greater than You

Navigating and going through a breakup creates soil for a rich spiritual journey, a connection to something greater (including your higher self—whatever that looks like for you). Maybe not the first week but over time, we naturally start looking up, in search of answers. Become curious to see more, to reevaluate our life and what it's all about. These are bigger questions than your pain. The same thing happens when we lose someone we loved. We can't make sense of it, so we look to the stars. We let go and let God. Or Buddha. Or whoever or whatever is greater. This releasing of our grip, being open to answers, is truly one of the strongest vines to pull you out of the quicksand.

When you look higher, you stop making it about yourself. Because you trust there was a reason. Pain without a reason is suffering. Pain with a reason is a chapter in your story, a jigsaw piece in the big puzzle that is your life. As long as you understand and believe that pain has a place in your story, that it's a piece in that puzzle, you'll experience more acceptance, peace, and letting go.

At this point you'll move past your own little world and start thinking universally. Your pain and suffering, your daily pleasures, your desire to be loved and wear designer jeans, all seem like options on a sports car instead of the engine. Life becomes about something greater, and seeking that something greater makes your problems small but your story big.

This is the shift. When you turn your dial from *what I'm going through* to *how will my story help others?*, you pull yourself out of your mental trenches. You're able to see beyond your current problems. Now you see there's a reason why you're here, going through what you're going through. And that reason is greater than you. You begin to understand that you're driving a car not just to move yourself around but to carry others. Your story will help others.

The "You Cheated/Left Me for Someone Else" Breakup

Infidelity is a complex terrain. It tells us about longing and loss, about our need for connection and autonomy, about our illusions of ownership and control, and about our conflicting desires for security and adventure.

—ESTHER PEREL

AUDREY AND ZAC

The way he stuffed her cat into a carrier and chucked the trash bags at the front door felt like an '80s movie—ridiculous and unbelievable. Audrey, who was about to turn the big three-0 that weekend, looked back at Zac as he wiped his runny nose on the sleeve of his AllSaints leather jacket she'd bought him just two weeks ago, then said something that would leave her completely confused.

"You're, like, preventing me from succeeding."

Inside, Audrey shattered like a plate thrown against a wall. On the outside, she was as calm as a cucumber—she'd always been good at not showing her cards—but inside her anxiety was shooting through the roof. Not even a bottle of Xanax could have tamed it. She couldn't show him that, though, because any type of negative reaction would just give him another reason to dump her.

So Audrey did what Audrey did best—bottled up her feelings and shoved them as far back into the darkness of her unconscious as she could in hopes that Zac would remember what a loving, cool, laid-back girlfriend she was, and had always been.

Inside swirled words that never surfaced.

All I have ever done is support you so you don't waste your "musical gifts." I mean, I took on an extra job that makes me hate my mornings so I can afford to pay all of your bills, so you can have more time to work on your fucking music! We live together—we've built a LIFE together. You can't be fucking serious, Zac.

Audrey threw the last trash bag into the backseat of her janky 1999 Toyota Corolla, buckled Mr. Jingles's crate in the passenger seat, and plopped herself in front of the steering wheel. Still trying to wrap her head around Zac's reasoning for ending the relationship.

She turned the key in the ignition and glanced back at their rented house one last time, secretly hoping he would run out screaming that he'd made a huge mistake. But he didn't.

Audrey sighed, wiped the mascara-mixed tears off her

face with a dirty In-N-Out napkin from their last date night, and drove off.

Now she could let her guard down. Sobbing and screaming, she sped down the 101 freeway. Replaying everything she could have said or done in the last four years to make Zac believe she was "preventing him from succeeding." In Audrey's eyes, she was nothing but a good girlfriend to Zac. She attended every single one of his shows, no matter how far or inconvenient they were for her and her schedule. She was the first person to listen to his music and always told him how great it was—even if she would rather have had her eardrums gouged out with a spoon than listen to another one of his terribly written songs. She paid his bills, washed his clothes, made sure his dinner was warm after long recording sessions, and woke him up with a blow job.

The fireworks had immediately gone off for both Zac and Audrey the second they laid eyes on each other at a concert. Neither had ever felt like that about someone before. They quickly became inseparable and moved in together after four months of dating.

Zac was Audrey's first real boyfriend. He wasn't like the other guys, who would pretend to be interested in a relationship only to ghost her after they finally had sex. Zac opened doors for her. Took her out on dates to restaurants that required reservations, not to bars at eleven o'clock at night. Made her a VIP at every one of his shows, wrote songs about their magnetic love, went down on her without being asked, and introduced her to his family very early on. He wanted a relationship, not just a hang and bang.

Audrey did whatever it took to avoid losing him. Even if that meant molding herself into the person she thought Zac wanted her to be.

It wasn't long before Audrey became codependent on Zac. She did whatever he wanted, whenever he wanted. His friends became her friends. His life became her life. His goals and dreams became her goals and dreams. If he wasn't happy, she wasn't happy. She neglected her own wants and needs in order to have enough energy to meet his. She put Zac on a tall marble pedestal while he left her on the cold dirt floor.

Audrey's phone rang, and she quickly snapped back to the present. She dug through her purse for it (trying not to merge into other cars going at least ninety miles per hour in the process). She answered it, hoping it was Zac calling to tell her he changed his mind and couldn't live without her . . .

It wasn't.

She cleared the lump in her throat before answering. It was her best friend, Kim. "Did you and Zac break up?"

That was strange. Audrey hadn't yet called, texted, or told anyone that Zac broke up with her. She cleared the lump in her throat again, trying to act like everything was fine when it wasn't.

"Uhhhh, I dunno. Kind of. Why?" Audrey's palms were sweaty, and she firmly gripped the steering wheel so her hands wouldn't slip off it.

Kim was hesitant, but finally said, "I think Zac has a new girlfriend." Audrey slammed on her brakes, shrieking "WHAT?!" And immediately got rear-ended by a Ford F-150.

It hadn't even been an hour since Zac broke up with her, and now Audrey was stewing on the side of the freeway and watching a tow truck drive off with her totaled car. So she did what every ex does shortly after a breakup, when they finally acknowledge a weird gut feeling they've had for a couple of weeks but were ignoring. She stalked his Instagram. And immediately regretted it.

Audrey noticed things she hadn't before. Zac didn't just have a new girlfriend—he'd been in a full-blown relationship. Audrey had blown off the numerous photos of the twenty-one-year-old super-fan before, but now, tracking through new lenses, she realized his "biggest fan" had been hanging out with him in real life, outside of concert venues. And of course, Audrey had met her. Many, many times.

"What a lying sack of shit." Those words surfaced, fast. Audrey felt humiliated. She closed the app and called Zac. But to no one's surprise, he had already blocked her number. *"FUCK!"*

Audrey debated throwing her phone into oncoming traffic, but instead she did the next best thing, what many people (who have never been to therapy) do after breakups: She texted every person with a penis in her contacts.

For the next couple of weeks, Audrey tried (a lot) to fuck the pain away (and failed). She was extremely determined to get even with Zac. Even if that meant lowering her standards and getting treated like shit by men she would never have given the time of day to if not for this hiatus. Yes, "hiatus."

In her mind, she was taking a break. She was not following her girlfriends' breakup advice, that the best way to get over someone is to get under somebody else, because this wasn't a breakup. She would get him back, she told herself. She would fix this. Right after this payback sex, which quickly came to an end after she picked up two STIs.

If this had really been an '80s movie, Audrey would have stood outside Zac's bedroom window wearing a trench coat and holding a boombox over her head that was playing their song—the one he wrote that she'd tried so hard to like. But it wasn't an '80s movie. Instead, she sent him long emails. Texted him. DM-ed him. Radio silence was the only response.

Zac had drawn firm boundaries, something Audrey would look back on many years later and thank him for because at the time she didn't have the strength to draw boundaries herself. She would also learn that it was Zac's new girlfriend, not Zac, who made the decision to cut her off. His new girlfriend was threatening to leave him if he communicated with Audrey in any form. (We can all guess how long that relationship lasted.)

Meanwhile, Audrey was revving in one gear—desperation. She needed to go higher, call on something greater. The universe. She decided she was going to "manifest" Zac returning to her by using the Law of Attraction. She left her house for the first time in weeks and spent hundreds of dollars she didn't have on books about the Law of Attraction so she could get Zac back sooner rather than later.

She got extremely excited for the first time in months and performed each ritual the books had to offer. She wrote love letters to Zac and burned them, made vision boards of their reunion, journaled as if they were still together, and put all her energy only toward dreaming about him leaving his new girlfriend for her. But nothing happened.

After months of manifesting and a pregnancy scare, Audrey finally gave up and accepted that it was over. She spent the next nine months isolated in her bedroom. Drinking hard liquor, smoking a lot of weed, and listening to every Taylor Swift album on repeat in hopes that the combination would either fill the gaping hole that was once her heart or entirely numb any emotion at all she might feel. It didn't. She stopped eating, exercising, bathing, or responding to her concerned friends' calls and texts. She lost her job, as well as a lot of weight, and relied on unemployment checks to (barely) pay her bills.

When Audrey wasn't sobbing about how unfair and awful her life was, she was obsessively stalking Zac's and his new girlfriend's social media. Zooming in on every inch of the girlfriend's face and body, trying to find as many flaws as she could so she wouldn't feel as shitty about herself. She would then blame herself for the relationship ending, becoming convinced that Zac was happier and healthier, that he treated the new girl way better than he ever treated her. Because that was the story their social media pages broadcast to the world.

As she looked on her phone at old photos and videos from their relationship, **she played the highlight reel instead of the documentary**. Romanticizing all the fun they had together, how perfect a couple they were. She would then call and cry to anyone who was willing to listen that Zac was "the one that got away" and she would never do better. This is when I usually get the call from someone seeking help. When their friends start sending them to voicemail.

But not Audrey. She needed to go to a darker place first. Sometimes you just can't avoid it. She wasn't ready to talk and process with a professional, because doing so would mean doing some work—looking at what happened through new lenses and taking ownership. She needed to feel what she needed to feel—to soak in her own bathwater. To eat chips until she felt sick to her stomach. To not shower until she couldn't stand her own smell.

Going this dark is better for the therapist as well. Clients who make it into the room because they bent to the pressure from friends and family to get help, but who aren't ready to do any work, just end up going through the motions and wasting a lot of time and money. It's better to catch the client on the bounce—when they're reeling from the latest setback. That's why sometimes you need to hit rock bottom. It's the only way to find out you can't live there.

Audrey needed to feel worthless, pathetic, and sorry for herself. She needed to hardly recognize herself in the mirror—to see the very depressed, frail, and sickly-looking person with no purpose or sense of self, who didn't know how she was going to get through this and who had replaced the once-vibrant, healthy-looking woman who liked herself and believed all people were good. She needed to feel like this condition was impossible to move on from. But most of all, she needed a few friends and family members to get together and read "We're worried about you" letters to her. That was the final straw. Nothing will make you realize where you're truly at as fast as an intervention. Audrey finally hit rock bottom.

WHAT REALLY HAPPENED

As I started doing sessions with Audrey, I learned that she had been through many breakups. But this one chopped her down at the knees. It was the first time someone had cheated on her, but it wasn't just the cheating. It was what the cheating activated—the false belief that she was not lovable. This false belief had also been the driving force behind her self-sacrificing behavior in the relationship. Her younger self had desperately wanted to prove she was lovable.

"He called you a piece of shit?" I asked.

"Among other things. Idiot, fat, ugly, loser."

These words didn't come from Zac. They were from her stepdad.

"And where was your mom?"

"Right next to him."

I felt sadness and rage. I imagined my own daughter as a teenager and wondered what would ever compel me to say those kinds of words to her. How badly would my life have to have gone? How much abuse must I have gone through in my own childhood to "pay it forward" like that? Then I thought about Audrey's mom and what kind of place she must have been in, about what kind of story she told herself to allow her husband's verbal abuse of her daughter to continue.

What Audrey didn't know was that her behavior in the relationship, intended to prove she was lovable—putting Zac on a pedestal, paying his bills, never saying no to him, bending over backwards for him, until she broke—had changed the dynamic of the relationship over time. She thought this was what a "good girlfriend" looked like, but Zac started to see her as clingy and controllable, more like an annoying sister than a partner. He lost respect for her. Of course, he wasn't aware of this dynamic happening beneath the surface, but it was what created drift, flipped the magnet, and led him to pursue others. The young groupie wasn't the only one. She was just the one he got caught with.

Maybe It Had Nothing to Do with You

If you're going through a "you cheated/left me for someone else" breakup, you're going to feel betrayal and rage. You're going to feel shocked and confused. Like the blindsided breakup, it will rock you like a hit-and-run. The difference here is internalization: there's more room for internalization when there's been infidelity. Even after all the feelings fade, the second and more dangerous punch keeps resounding: *Was it because of me? Maybe I didn't love them well enough. Maybe I'm bad in bed. Maybe they left because I gained ten pounds. Is there something wrong with me?*

When someone cheats on you, it's very different than if the relationship had fallen apart because of conflict that couldn't be resolved, or because the two of you drifted too far apart to turn back (your feelings changed). When your partner cheats on you, it's easy to point the finger at yourself, to assume, *I'm not enough. I'm defective.* You question your worth more than your behavior. Now, it's not about love but about self-love. *Do I have value as a person? Am I worthy of healthy love? Did I deserve to be cheated on?*

Audrey tied her worth to Zac and the relationship. Unconsciously, she wanted to prove that she had value, that she was in fact lovable. As I mentioned already, this was the driving force behind her behavior as she did everything she could to be a "good girlfriend" and keep Zac happy. So her discovery that Zac had cheated brought up this false belief about being unlovable and fixed a harsh spotlight on it. She was not in fact a good girlfriend. Because she was not lovable.

This false belief was why it was so hard for Audrey to let go. If she could get Zac back, then it would mean she was lovable. Getting him back had less to do with wanting Zac himself and more to do with proving she had value. Read that again. Because chances are you, like Audrey, wouldn't want someone back who's cheated on you. But we all want to prove we have value. This is why breaking up with Zac was the toughest breakup Audrey had ever been through.

Again, it wasn't about love. It was about self-love. Ask yourself if you are internalizing after being cheated on. If so, what does that look like? Ask yourself what false beliefs about yourself are being activated because of being cheated on. What are you telling yourself about your worth because of someone else's behavior and choices?

When Audrey realized that the breakup with Zac was less about losing a relationship and more about trying to prove she was lovable, she was finally able to let go. This is when her lenses changed. She saw what was really happening and why she kept chasing after him. Although she still spent many sleepless nights crying about Zac, she stopped sinking in her feelings and spinning in her distorted thoughts—or as I would say, she stopped swimming in her own shit. She also stopped drinking and smoking weed, and she switched up the repeating Taylor Swift albums. Audrey slowly accepted that her relationship with Zac had "expired," and she stopped thinking about all the what-ifs. She finally drew boundaries with Sharpie instead of chalk by deleting Zac's number and blocking his social media pages. She blocked his new girlfriend on every platform as well.

Audrey took a much-needed break from dating and casual sex so she could start to learn to be with herself and stop tying her value to another person. She burned the love letters, vision boards, and dream journals of her imagined reunion with Zac. She threw out all her books on the Law of Attraction and replaced them with books on codependency, trauma, and attachment style instead.

She started eating again and gained back all the weight she had lost. She moved her body through her grief by picking up yoga, meditation, and her new favorite hobby—rock climbing. She went back to school to study business and got a job at an animal shelter. She practiced being kind to herself, especially on her bad days, by treating herself to an expensive vibrator and giving herself orgasms often. Getting to know her body for the first time. Not to mention allowing herself to indulge with large chocolate milkshakes every "Fuck It Friday"—like I do.

Zac slowly became a distant memory, and the sting of betrayal subsided. Audrey was finally on a path to healing and was completely invested in herself. She felt something she thought would never happen in a million years: she was happy. And happy on her own, not in a relationship with someone else. When Zac finally reached out two years after the breakup, telling her, "I miss you," she never responded.

After hitting rock bottom and working on herself, Audrey had realized that Zac's cheating had nothing to do with her. Yes, the relationship dynamic and chemistry might have changed, but that wasn't just because of her. She was only 50 percent of the story. The relationship changed because they both failed to look at themselves, to communicate their state and feelings and inner journey, and to talk about how that made the relationship skip off the tracks. When it did, neither of them did anything about it.

Audrey realized that it wasn't all her fault. Yes, she contributed to changes in the relationship, but Zac's choices were his own. Not hers. And those choices had to do with his tools, his story, and his insecurity, ego, and impulsivity. This realization was what freed her. From there, she no longer internalized and was able to review the relationship with fresh eyes. Audrey could finally begin the process that would truly empower her—taking ownership (which we'll get into in the chapter on break-through work).

Common Reasons People Cheat

It may be helpful to see that there was a reason for your partner's cheating. And that reason may have nothing to do with you. It also didn't just come out of nowhere. It came from somewhere, even if it was just an impulse. Impulsivity may have been a pattern of behavior. Maybe compounded by the situation or by drift, whether in the relationship or within self. As you mull over being cheated on, it may also be helpful to see your ex as a person, not a monster.

In general, there are six reasons why people cheat:

1. **Anger or Revenge**

   Some cheat as an act of revenge. For example, if one partner has been flirting with someone or even cheating, the other partner may cheat as well as a form of payback.

   Anger-driven infidelity may be driven by:

   - Frustration when your partner doesn't understand you or your needs
   - Anger at a partner who is never around
   - Anger at a partner who doesn't seem to contribute to the relationship
   - Anger or frustration after an argument

All these are reactions to feelings that are unprocessed and have not been communicated to the partner. These feelings may have very little or nothing to do with the partner and what they bring to the table.

2. **Falling Out of Love**

The excitement, passion, and exhilaration of the initial phase of a relationship usually fade over time. The rush of dopamine drops. This is normal in every relationship. And I say it's when the love truly begins, because it's when we have to work through our differences, look at ourselves and our patterns, and build something sustainable. But many do not do that. Instead, believing the love isn't there anymore, they end up cheating. Simply put, they cheat because they don't want to do the work.

3. **Feeling Unappreciated**

If one partner feels neglected or undervalued in a relationship, they may begin to yearn for those needs to be met. Yes, we have a responsibility to fill our own cup (meet our own foundational needs), like feeling worthy and attractive and having our own life outside of our relationship. But feeling seen, heard, desired, and respected are legit relationship needs (as in things needed for a relationship to thrive). When they go unmet for long enough, many start looking elsewhere to have those needs satisfied.

4. **Lack of Commitment**

People with commitment issues are more likely to cheat in their relationship, whether because they have a fear of intimacy or abandonment or because they believe the grass is always greener on the other side. Whatever the reason, they simply struggle with commitment. Some reasons for commitment-related infidelity may include:

- Difference of opinion about whether the relationship should be casual or exclusive
- Fear of committing even to a partner they love
- Fear of intimacy
- Fear of abandonment that leads to not committing for too long or to sabotaging the relationship
- Not feeling worthy of healthy love or not believing they can love in a healthy way

5. **Sexual Desire**

   For some people, infidelity doesn't always spell relationship trouble or unhappiness. Their cheating is simply the result of sexual desire, even if they are happy and fulfilled in their relationship. Some other reasons for infidelity driven by sexual desire include:

- Feeling unsatisfied with sex within the relationship
- A desire to try something new
- A desire to express kinks and fetishes
- Very different sex drives
- A desire to explore sexuality in ways their partner has no desire for

Of course, none of these reasons make cheating okay. There should be conversations about differing desires and exploration of desires together. However, someone who just wants to have sex may look for opportunities to do so without any other reason.

6. Situational Opportunity

Infidelity sometimes happens because a partner was in a situation where the opportunity presented itself. But remember, they may also have been primed to cheat, for any of the reasons listed here. The situation just made it easy for them. Maybe they got drunk with a co-worker who they already felt close to and had some chemistry with and maybe they were also drifting in their relationship at home. Or maybe they resented or were angry at their partner. Or their emotional needs weren't getting met. Again, none of these reasons made it okay to cheat. But someone who never intended to cheat might do so in a situation that makes it much easier to do so.

Here are some other situational factors that may induce someone to cheat:

- Being in a long-distance relationship
- Being on vacation
- Wanting physical comfort after a distressing event
- Living or working in an environment that encourages closeness and emotional connection

BREAK-THROUGH WORK
Take Your Agency Back

You've allowed yourself to feel all the feelings—anger, rage, sadness, etc.—and you've started to process what happened, to accept it, to let go, and to stop internalizing. The riptide has passed, your emotional waves are calming down, and you can see the sun again. You've drawn boundaries, you're protecting yourself, and you've started therapy (hopefully). Now you're ready for the final and most important step: taking ownership.

If you're feeling defensive as you're reading this, I get it. After all, you weren't the one who cheated. But ownership doesn't mean it was your fault. Taking ownership is acknowledging that you're 50 percent of any relationship, and that you've contributed to the relationship dynamic in some way, maybe by not expressing your needs. Ownership is how you take your agency back.

Many skip this step and default to victim mode. They believe that something happened *to* them, and they become angry and untrusting and afraid to love again. They create their own prison.

You have to be really honest with yourself and decide when you're ready for this step. It's a crucial step to take if you're going to break through.

Here's what Audrey started to own. Remembering every fight and all the dysfunction that was deeply embedded in the relationship. Seeing the red flags. Like when Zac stopped kissing her during sex six months in. Or when she had to look the other way as he got overly flirty with his fangirls at his shows . . . or any attractive girl who crossed his path. Because if she didn't look the other way, then she was "jealous," "crazy," or "insecure." Just like his exes before her. Or when he never bought her flowers because, in his eyes, she "wasn't the type of girl men buy flowers for." Or when the spontaneous road trips to his shows never actually were much fun and always ended in explosive fights that drove him to disappear and not return the next day.

She saw that she had minimized all this behavior and stayed mute, not expressing her struggles with the relationship. She loved *around* Zac instead of *with* him. Audrey realized she had allowed herself to be a doormat in their relationship. She had ignored her own wants, needs, and concerns because she didn't believe she deserved to have them. Or that she could do better than Zac. She just wanted to be loved. And to be loved by Zac, she had to remain silent.

That's what she owned: that her silence contributed to Zac treating her the way he did. That was her part, what she contributed to the relationship dynamic. She certainly didn't make him cheat by being unable to speak up. His cheating was *not* her fault. Zac's cheating was on him, and no one but Zac could know exactly why he did it. Most likely, if he ever chose to do the work, he would have to dig deep and reflect, since there are always many layers to cheating. But Audrey did contribute to the relationship dynamic, and that contribution was hers to own.

Owning it also showed her what she needed to work on. For herself. For her relationship with herself (to build self-worth) and ultimately for what she would bring to the table in her next relationship.

What are some things you want to own in your expired relationship? Did you also not speak up? Did you allow unhealthy behavior because you were afraid of losing your partner? Or scared of being alone? Did you, like Audrey, believe you didn't deserve better? Take a minute and think (or write in your journal) about what you are now ready to own for the ending of the relationship. Not for your ex cheating, but for what you contributed to the relationship dynamic. Think about patterns from other relationships. How did the way you showed up, or didn't, contribute to the drift, the conflict, the disconnect, or the death of the relationship?

The more Audrey started to own her part in the relationship dynamic with Zac—meaning, when she started to heal—the clearer her lenses became. She saw things she hadn't seen before. When we take ownership, we create distance and we're able to take a wider view. When we're in victim mode, we can't see anything. We can only cast blame, which narrows our lenses. By owning her piece, Audrey started to see that Zac wasn't as great and charming a boyfriend as she'd thought he was. He was manipulative, emotionally abusive, and an excellent gaslighter—which felt familiar to Audrey because so was her stepfather. She learned that her attraction to Zac wasn't chemistry. It was a trauma bond. That's why the breakup took a major toll on her mental health.

All this was validating for Audrey to finally understand. She could now afford to see a therapist (me) weekly. She went out with her friends, tried new things, picked up hobbies, and created new love experiences. When she started to date again, she could finally see her growth. She noticed that she wasn't as clingy, and if she was rejected, she didn't define herself by it but told herself, "It just wasn't a good fit." She practiced setting boundaries and expressing her needs to men. It felt uncomfortable, and not everyone created space for it. But she knew that speaking up from the start would weed out the people who weren't good for her. It would prevent her from meeting another Zac and repeating old unhealthy love patterns.

Audrey strived to do her best every day and didn't settle for less than what she wanted and deserved. For the first time in her life, she believed she had worth. She believed she was lovable. Of course, she still had bad days, and sometimes she felt heartbroken over short-lived relationships that didn't work out. But those breakups didn't destroy her. And she never allowed these men to define her value or sense of self like she used to do.

I checked in with Audrey a year later, after the dust had settled and she had healed some. I wanted to know what the positive and negative impacts were of what happened. Here's what she said:

The positive is definitely that it sent me to therapy. If he had never cheated, I probably would have continued to date similar people and have continued to be my toxic insecure self. I would have always, as you say, tied the relationship to my worth, making my relationships lopsided and myself powerless. It forced me to look at myself instead of hiding behind others and recognize my worth. It made me realize that being lovable had to do with my relationship with self, not my relationship to others.

The negative is I definitely struggle with trust issues and it really activated my fear of abandonment. I thrive when I'm single, but the second I meet someone, I, like, get filled with fear and anxiety. I get super hypervigilant too and want to run the second I see one "red flag" that reminds me of my ex who cheated. Social media is also triggering if the guy I'm dating likes another girl's photo or anything like that—but that's all my shit I still need to work on.

Like most of my clients who have been cheated on, the gold for Audrey was the awakening. It was the purpose of her "hero's journey": returning to the village (herself) a changed person. What's hard is to learn how to trust again, to love without fear. Of course, this takes time and many more new love experiences to eclipse the old one.

But is learning to trust a new issue, or was it always there? Buried below the surface only to erupt when the relationship hit turbulence or expired? I find that, for most clients, what they now see has always been there and the breakup is the catalyst that surfaces what was hidden. So it can finally be what gets them to face and work through what they need to work through. Our breakups can become a black light.

But What About the Fucking Betrayal?!!!

Cheating is a monumental breach of trust that can keep us stuck. Unable to peel away the thick layer of betrayal. It's what can make this type of breakup more difficult than the others. Focusing on the lie, the broken promise, the backstabbing, the double cross. And the more we feed that, the harder it is to see any good in the relationship. Sitting in the feelings of betrayal is like a total eclipse that doesn't allow any light in. We sit in darkness, stewing in rage.

But the cheating wasn't just about the lying. Beneath the betrayal, something else was taken from you. Your worth. Your value. Your self-respect. The growing belief that you're lovable.

As I mentioned before, when someone cheats on you, it's easy to internalize. Not only do you wonder what you did wrong, but you wonder what's wrong with you. *Am I not enough? Am I unlovable? Am I bad in bed? Is it my feet?* You can start to believe you are defective. This feeling of being less than can be what drives you to get your ex back, as Audrey tried to do. Because, if you can get them back, it means you *are* enough. You're lovable, a great partner, and whatever insecurities you struggle with will go away. This is why letting go can be so difficult. You're not just letting go of a person. You're letting go of yourself. Your identity, your value, and all that you could be.

Here's the mindset to cultivate: being cheated on can be what you need to spark your becoming. Yes, there is a whole lot of pain and panic to endure and a long dark tunnel to crawl through. But on the other side, you will discover love patterns, possibly new non-negotiables, and what you need to work on. All of it for you.

Cheating is information. It's truth. It's an awakening. And not just for you, but for the person who was unfaithful as well. As Dr. Robert Weiss says, "For some, cheating on one's partner is a way to explore repressed parts of their self." Behind every betrayal is an unmet need. The truth is, they didn't cheat because their partner couldn't fulfill their needs. *They cheated on their partner because they couldn't fulfill their own needs.*

Your ex's cheating was telling of where your ex was at. It was something your ex did to you only if you choose to see it that way. If you see it only as premeditated, calculated betrayal, you will default to being a victim, your heart will harden, and the breakup will keep you from loving fearlessly. The "betrayal" will always have power over you.

The goal is to get yourself out of victim mode (the deep ditch). And the first step is to not see being cheated on solely as something purposely done to you, as a betrayal. It was your ex's response to something, a way of coping, perhaps. A numbing, a running away. A disconnection and reaction to a wounding.

When you're ready, taking some responsibility for the relationship dynamic is where things begin to tip and you move into empowerment. Again, the breakup may not have been your fault, but you contributed to the dynamic, even if it was the pattern of choosing this type of person, because you're 50 percent of any relationship.

Of course, claiming ownership takes time. You have to go through the feels. It may be necessary for you to sit in that ditch for a while. And that's okay. Cast blame. Point fingers. You have a right to do that. Someone hurt you. You trusted someone with your heart and they dropped it. But eventually you have to be able to climb out of the ditch. And the only way to do that is to own your responsibility.

In what ways did you overlook your personal values,

boundaries, and needs in order to maintain the relationship? Recognize patterns. Consider any recurring patterns in past relationships that may have contributed to the dynamic of this one. Did that relationship dynamic have any impact on the drift or the infidelity? Did the cheating change your identity or definition of self? Did you contribute to drift by not being present in the relationship? If so, how? Did you stop working on yourself? Your health, mind, and body? Your passion and your happiness? If so, how did that neglect ripple into the relationship? Finally, what are you holding on to that you need to let go of?

Experiencing betrayal activates the brain's stress response and triggers the release of stress hormones like cortisol—creating high levels of anxiety and emotional distress. The brain areas associated with social pain, such as the anterior cingulate cortex, can also become activated in ways similar to how they would respond to physical pain. Additionally, the prefrontal cortex, responsible for decision-making and emotional regulation, may be affected, potentially leading to difficulty in processing emotions and making rational decisions. The long-term effects of betrayal can diminish your ability to trust and can change how you perceive and engage in relationships. Because you're afraid to get burned again, you may believe the love stove is always hot, even though it's off.

Of course, not all breakups from infidelity play out this way. Some people are able to leave the relationship with no internal injuries. They're able to see the cheating as something like an accident that wasn't their fault. They know it had nothing to do with them and what they brought to the table. They understand that the betrayal had more to do with their partner's story than with theirs. Not all of us have this kind of clarity and security.

But is it true security? Infidelity has a long tail and many faces. It's usually not an impulsive act while drinking too much at a party, though of course that happens too. But usually being underwhelmed by a partner's cheating comes from drift in the relationship and feeling disconnected, both from each other and from self. Those who are not shaken by being cheated on and who move on fast may not be ready to take an honest look at self.

Infidelity and its impact on us is complicated and unique to our own story and where we're at in our life in our relationship with ourselves. If we have a poor and insecure relationship with self, we have a higher chance of internalizing and believing we are the reason our partner cheated— because we are defective in some way. No one wants to believe this, so either we try to get our partner back to prove the problem is not us, compromising ourselves and our self-worth, or we stay in blame mode, lock our pointed finger at "the cheater," and take zero responsibility.

You may not be guilty of the crime. But you were an accomplice in some way, even if it was just by deciding to look the other way (not addressing signs of relationship drift). Not acknowledging your role creates prison walls and a very deep ditch. You now believe that everyone's a cheater and you cannot fully trust anyone. Instead, you love from a distance. Showing only parts of yourself, not all of yourself.

Falling forward instead of back with your eyes closed and arms folded. This kind of untrusting love will always create only surface love, which ultimately dissolves like sugar in warm water. This becomes your pattern and you stop believing that real love exists. Because you have yet to experience it. For you, love is now a myth, right up there with Santa Claus and the Easter Bunny.

Your Friends Don't Know What You Need

In spite of their good intentions, the messages we get from friends and family after being cheated on can be damaging. *He did you wrong—fuck him. You deserve better. She's a piece of shit.* The world is on your side, but that's not always helpful. Turning your ex into a monster doesn't help you or your healing. It throws you into a victim mode ditch. Instead of villainizing your ex and stamping "urgent and high priority" on your forehead, they should stamp "fragile: handle with care" and treat you accordingly. Everyone wants to save you. But they're not taking a beat and allowing you to lead and go at your own pace.

You may have a friend who was also cheated on, but that doesn't make your situation the same as theirs. Chances are that this friend will be projecting their unhealed wounds onto you. Remember that no relationship is the same as another and infidelity is complicated. As Esther Perel says, "If the painful disclosure of the parallel love is to lead to a more honest future—for either one of the relationships involved—the other person needs to be treated as a human being. This should be done with care and respect. The lover needs support, not judgement, and might also need to explore rebuilding self esteem."

When your eleven-year-old child comes home broken-hearted because the "love of my life" said no when she asked him to the winter dance, you don't try to hook her up with her friends. You give her ice cream and sit with her and validate her feelings. With adult friends and family members, though, we come *at* them instead of staying *with* them. We turn our dial from heart-centered to solution-based. We forget that hearts are hearts no matter how old we are.

So take the beat before the bounce. It will be better for you and your relationship with self. Ask yourself what you need right now. Don't listen to what others think you need. Don't listen to people who have "been there before" unless what they are offering you is what you believe you need (and that's not advice). Who do you need to surround yourself with and who do you need to send to voicemail for a while?

After my divorce, I took a few weeks to feel sorry for myself. I locked my door, ordered in. I didn't shower. I Netflix-ed and slept. I didn't respond to texts other than to let people know I was alive and okay. I played the relationship back. I cried. A lot. I felt all the feelings—anger, regret, guilt, hopelessness, love, and hate.

I allowed myself to fall because I knew what was waiting for me when I was ready. The world telling me I needed to get up and find someone new. I wasn't ready to hear that. So I went to therapy. Did burpees. Ran on the beach and rode my motorcycle. I dropped into my body and gave it calm and stillness. I spent a lot of time alone and went to dark places. But I knew I wasn't running or numbing. Going to dark places can be what's needed to reset, reboot, reenergize, before swimming back to the surface. Because when you get to the surface, you have to swim to the island—and you now have an audience.

But eventually you do have to come up. The oxygen tank has a limited supply. You can't live forever at the bottom. Staying there too long can bring on addictions, unhealthy behavior patterns, and a crippling depression. I ate doughnuts. But not the entire box. You have to know yourself. Going dark is okay. As long as you set a timer.

Note: If you don't have friends and family and a support system waiting for you when you're ready, falling for any amount of time may not be healthy for you. If your breakup was devastating and you feel yourself isolating, it may be wise to get into a therapy room as soon as possible. It won't be a good idea to go into dark spaces. You have to know yourself. For example, if you're an extrovert, surrounding yourself with handpicked friends may be the beat you need. If you're an introvert, like me, being alone can be medicine. Be honest with yourself. Give yourself what you truly believe you need.

Reminder

The behavior of cheating has more to do with the cheater, their story, and where they're at in their life than it does with you.

The Soap Opera Breakup

"I Need to Get a Restraining Order"

Embrace the turmoil, for it leads to a newfound sense of
self and the promise of a brighter future beyond the storm.
—ANONYMOUS

SUSAN AND DARREN

Susan met Darren in her midtwenties in New York City, where good friends and a fresh "everything" bagel were all she needed to feel reset after a one-night stand and three hours of sleep. Where waking up with someone you didn't like wasn't that big a deal. It was just Tuesday, and the fact that he lived two blocks from her work made it worth it. Susan was a bartender and Darren was a musician. The magic moment, the moment she knew, was when he came back, out of breath, after getting her number. She was bartending a private party in the penthouse of a twelve-story building.

The elevator was jammed, so he used the stairs, after realizing she only gave him nine digits.

With its bone-chilling cold, high rent, and emotionally unstable roommates, New York, the trauma bonding capital of the world, was where two-ply toilet paper and finding yourself were luxuries and survival mode was homeostasis. A place where a month-to-month lifestyle created the perfect petri dish for every young person who packed their Pontiac Sunfire and left their small town and dysfunctional family for a higher life and a harder fall. As you can guess, Susan and Darren's love story was pretty textbook. Love between an alcoholic and a codependent bartender living in a four-hundred-square-foot apartment came with an expiration date.

They were together for ten years, a long roller-coaster of *I love you*s and *Get away*s. Intermittent love and fighting so loud that windows had to be closed, even in New York. But the Taurus in Susan kept her from leaving. Until she started breaking up with herself.

Darren went on tours, and Susan needed to know she was desirable again. That's when she noticed Wade, her favorite barista. He paid attention to her, noticed little things, like the accented accessories to her outfits and the different ways she would wear her hair.

Susan knew she would get caught. It was just a matter of time. That's why she kept lying and going over to Wade's. It wasn't that he used sex toys on her, something Darren never did because he believed "real men don't need help." It had nothing to do with her new body-shaking orgasms, which before she'd always thought women did for attention. It had nothing to do with the sex at all actually, although from the outside it would appear that way. It was her way out of something she felt trapped in—her ten-year relationship.

Although Darren had a short fuse, he wasn't much of a fighter. All bark, zero bite. His last fight was in seventh grade, when he swung at a smaller kid so he would look tough in front of the bigger boys. It lasted two and a half seconds and he cried the entire walk home.

Knowing Darren wasn't a fighter was why Susan pulled up in a cab in front of their apartment with Wade. She knew Darren would be waiting for her. She'd left way too many clues. It was perfect. She could kill two birds with one stone: breaking up with Wade, because she no longer needed to prove to herself that she was desirable, and also breaking up with Darren after he caught her with someone else. Finally, everyone would be able to go their separate ways.

But there was one thing Susan didn't consider. Darren's drinking problem made him not only fearless but stupid. When he saw Susan getting out of the cab, Darren rushed out of the apartment with the kind of certainty Susan hadn't seen in him in years, grabbed Wade out of the cab, and started whaling on him without missing a beat. As if he had rehearsed this encounter a thousand times in his head. When the cabdriver tried to break it up, Darren punched him as well. It turned into a bloody mess and Susan just stood there in shock.

It wasn't supposed to play out like this. Darren was supposed to flip her off and go to a bar. And Wade was supposed to see the guilt and shame etched on Susan's face and know that his "Mrs. Robinson" fantasy was over. But instead, it all backfired. Susan felt horrible. But she also felt something else.

"I felt closer to Darren that night than I had in years," she admitted.

In this, our fifth session, it finally all came out. The affair. The street fight. The plan that went south. All within the first twenty minutes. In the first four sessions we had covered her career and lopsided friendships and other random things. She obviously wasn't ready to talk about what she'd come to see me for. I would politely probe about her relationship, but she would sway the conversation away.

As a therapist, you have to make sure you meet the client where they're at. It's their session. Clients can talk about anything they want. But at the same time, it's a therapist's job to guide, to challenge, and often to confront, using questions as a rudder to steer conversations. If not, there's just a lot of bird walking and a bored client. Some clients blame it on the therapist and say that therapy isn't working for them. And some therapists terminate, thinking there's nothing to process.

But nothing *is* something. There is no such thing as bird walking. It all matters. It's all true and valid and meaningful, and it all must come out, consciously or unconsciously, for other things to come out. It's all part of the process, as they say. I get that. But I also think letting a client talk too long about only the easy stuff is a way to hide, avoid, and stall. So you have to meet clients where they're at and wait them out until things surface. And when they do, things unravel pretty fast.

"It was the first time he had ever fought for the relationship," I confirmed. "In this case, literally."

"Yeah," Susan agreed. "It turned me on kinda."

"It gave you hope."

"It confused me."

To see something in Darren she thought wasn't there anymore was so confusing that it even made her feel a little crazy. As though she couldn't trust herself anymore. Suddenly Susan felt like maybe she was wrong. Maybe this wasn't over. Maybe they could try couples counseling again and turn this relationship around. She would work on her conflict avoidance and codependency, and he could work on his drinking problem and his ability to show emotions and actually be present in the relationship. Maybe with therapy both of them would "get their shit together." No more lies. No more cheating. This could be the reset they needed. A new beginning.

But Darren didn't see it that way. He was actually done. He'd had a different revelation that night. He was with the wrong person. He deserved someone who could have honest conversations instead of staging blowups. The relationship was over. He ended it with Susan and checked into a rehab shortly after.

The rehab was a plug-and-play enabling Darren to move on. He had structure, new friends, and three process groups a day. He got obsessed with working on himself. Susan knew this because she read his raw and inspiring posts about his recovery journey on social media. She was quite surprised he could write so well. But more importantly, she noticed his new ability to be vulnerable and truly show himself. This was the result of sobriety. Everything she wanted him to be was happening right in front of her eyes. Without her.

He shared his story, grew a following, and started to help others as a sober coach. He now had a sense of purpose, something he'd never had before. As Susan told me this in our session, I knew exactly what Darren was experiencing. I had gone through the same process after my divorce, and I knew the path he was on. Secretly I was rooting for him. He had found his cape. When someone finds meaning and a sense of purpose, they become unstoppable. Darren was long gone from Susan and their relationship.

But Susan felt like a stepping-stone. The next person would get the 2.0 version of Darren after she had lived for ten years with the shitty beta. This feeling is common after breakups. Many of my clients feel the way Susan did when they see their ex finally thriving and becoming the person they always wanted to be with. It's crushing when you realize that you were the catalyst for their evolution. Feeling ripped off and used only adds to your anger. Not only did you experience the emotional roller-coaster of living with them before they got it together, but your life was sacrificed for them to become a better human.

"It's fucking bullshit!" Susan announced in our final session. As she was ranting about how unfair all this was, I couldn't help but think about my ex-wife. I remember she felt the same way. I couldn't hear it at the time. All I knew was that she left me. *Too bad*. She was the one who wanted a divorce, not me. But as Susan broke down in tears, explaining how she felt like her entire relationship with Darren was a waste of all that she had sacrificed for them, I felt what my ex-wife had felt. For the first time since my divorce fourteen years ago, I felt empathy and compassion for her. I didn't have an alcohol problem, but I didn't even know how to load a dishwasher. I was a man-child who was jealous, controlling, and unhappy and did nothing about it. I was holding her hostage and calling it love.

Unlike Darren, though, Wade wasn't done. For Wade, it wasn't just about sex. He had fallen in love with Susan. To be fair, she had been seeing him off and on for a year! Susan had told Wade that she was in a relationship with him, that she had broken up with Darren years ago. (She just didn't tell Darren.) Wade met her emotional needs. He listened to her and made her feel seen. This was why she was having earth-shaking orgasms. It had nothing to do with the sex toys.

But even though she felt desired and valued, Susan wasn't in love with Wade. He was too young. His socks rarely matched. He didn't make his bed. But being with him had proved to her that it was possible to feel desirable and valued. And that she wasn't crazy or asking for too much. But again, it was her resistance to conflict and expressing her wants, her inability to have hard conversations, that kept Wade and her going. Not love.

She finally broke this pattern with Wade. She ended the affair. She actually talked to him, was finally honest with him, told him they couldn't be together. It wasn't what she had wanted, and Wade deserved something real. Not to be someone's shot of validation. This was the first time in Susan's life that she drew hard lines. But it backfired. And so began the kind of crazy you see in movies and read about in secret Facebook groups.

Wade stalked her. Left notes on her doorstep. Made fake social media accounts so he could follow and message her. Interrogated her friends. Susan was so confused. She'd done everything she was supposed to do, but it didn't work. Wade wasn't going away. She ignored him, but ignoring a child only throws fuel on his fire. He did all the things that people who haven't worked on their abandonment issues do. Grabbing. Clinging. Reacting.

Wade didn't know this because he wasn't in therapy. He didn't know that his behavior had nothing to do with Susan or love or the relationship. Connecting her leaving with his worth, he was willing to take any measure to prove he had value, that he was lovable—messages he did not receive as a child. As his attempts to get her back continued, Susan, feeling that her life was turning into a creepy thriller, did what everyone (including me) encouraged her to do: she blocked and unfollowed Wade on social media, and eventually, when he wouldn't stop doing everything he could to contact her, she filed for a restraining order.

Wade never physically harmed Susan, but for anyone, having to look over your shoulder daily and live in constant fear is just as damaging to your quality of life. Susan felt that Wade's harassment was some kind of punishment from God for cheating on Darren. She got the message, even said it out loud. Now she just wanted it to stop.

And one day it did. An eerie silence ensued, with no emails, no texts, no neighbors saying they saw him snooping around and she should be concerned. Wade had disappeared. Just like that. No warning, no announcement. Poof. Gone. Susan thought either her prayers were answered or he had hurt himself. She didn't care which it was. She was just happy the chaos stopped. Over time she stopped looking over her shoulder, and she went back to her life. Back to the gym, museums, and walks around the park.

Then she experienced something strange: loneliness, a deep loneliness that she had never felt before. She realized in a session that she had always had some kind of drama or chaos in her life. In a way, drama was what gave her life. Before Darren and Wade, it was her family. But now that there was nothing awful going on, life felt, "well, excruciating."

So of course she became curious about what Darren was up to. She stalked him on social media and saw a new man evolving and growing. He had a brand-new life. All she had were new door locks and a collection of therapists. (I believe I was number five.)

It took a few months for Susan to finally get up on one knee from the one-two punch of this double breakup. Sitting in her loneliness was brutal. I know I mentioned that therapists aren't supposed to tell their clients what to do. In this case, though, I told her exactly what to do. *Do not contact Darren. Don't make it about you. It's not fair to him and the journey he is on. You must sit in this loneliness to break the pattern of wanting chaos in your life. It's the only way you will truly know yourself, discover yourself, and like yourself. It's what happened to me.*

She took in that advice. Got back to the basics—sleep, nutrition, movement. She wanted to run, calling it "travel," but I encouraged her to stay put, to sit in her own bathwater. For once. If she were to run, she would only be running away from herself. And all the work we were doing would be wasted. She stayed. And I helped her find life in her life (more on this later). Four months on, she finally had the energy and willpower to unfollow and unfriend Darren, to stop messaging him and stalking him on social media. She cut the cord. And that was what kept her afloat and moving.

Following his surprisingly quick reinvention of himself had kept Susan's mind spinning in circles and kept her feeling heavy emotions that had her playing the highlight reel instead of the documentary (a crucial step I discuss later). This created false hope and a lot of what-ifs that kept her mentally and emotionally trapped. She had always wanted children someday, and Darren was her last chance at not having a "geriatric" pregnancy. (Thirty-five is officially considered geriatric, which is absurd and damaging.) But she didn't focus on what could be, only on what was. Still, Susan eventually took what she had in her life and found nectar and beauty. After spending a lot of time by herself, getting to know herself, she smashed the internal ticking clock and built a new life. From the inside out.

Darren came back around, like they always do. The girl he was dating turned out to be a rebound, and the wheels fell off his sobriety after they broke up. By then, Susan was in a very different place. The dust had settled, and she had new lenses. She wasn't interested in a round two. The only thing playing in her head was the documentary. Her radar was sharp, and she knew she needed to be alone for a while longer. But more importantly, she was strong enough now to do that.

Hint: If your ex starts dating someone relatively quickly after the expiration, know that it probably won't last. Space and distance are required after a breakup to learn, process, and grow from what happened. If you or your ex get into another relationship fast, you're jumping from one lily pad to another without the stretch of the swim. The richest soil for growth is when a relationship ends, and starting a new relationship so soon wastes that soil and prevents you from learning about your contribution to the ship sinking (baggage). It doesn't matter whose fault it was. You were 50 percent of the relationship, so you contributed to the expiration in some way, even if only by enabling. That contribution, if not examined, will carry over into the next relationship.

This is something we don't think about when an ex jumps right into a new relationship. Instead, we just feel shitty about ourselves because they found love again and we didn't. We feel like the kid who got held back or left behind. But the truth is, they probably did *not* find love. Love is built and earned and takes time. Your ex was probably going to their plan B: finding some comfort and probably satisfying some skin hunger by finding someone who gave them attention, someone to lose themselves in. So they didn't have to face what they needed to work on. Again.

WHAT REALLY HAPPENED

Susan didn't cheat to get caught and be free from the relationship. That's what was on the surface. Underneath, she cheated to save Darren. It was the only way to maybe force him to look at himself. It was her only chance to try to change someone who didn't want to change.

Darren's band had kicked him out, and he had fallen into a depression, which led to more drinking. He needed to hit rock bottom to start looking inward and heal childhood traumas and wounds. Getting kicked out of his band didn't do it. So Susan created his rock bottom for him. She developed a relationship with Wade because the codependent in her was trying to save Darren's life. Yes, it felt good to be wanted and desired. But it wasn't about Wade or about wanting to leave the relationship. The relationship had ended years ago. She was now just trying to save Darren.

Sometimes we unconsciously map things to happen that we're not even aware of. These things are happening under the surface, and if we're not in therapy unearthing and processing the unconscious, our conscious awareness can make us believe something else. That she was actually trying to save Darren, more than herself, was a huge revelation for Susan. It helped her be more compassionate with herself and her actions but also reminded her of how ingrained her codependency was. She was reminded of the work she needed to do on herself.

All breakups require meaning. We try to make sense of them, to connect the dots to get some kind of closure and acceptance. To move toward acceptance by discovering what else was happening that we didn't realize, what was going on that was greater than ourselves. And no other kind of breakup requires seeking meaning more than the chaotic toxic breakup.

Yes, being blindsided can leave you with missing puzzle pieces. And not seeing the complete picture can cause you to internalize. But you can get to a place where you realize that your ex's action was a reaction and a way of coping, that it was more about them than you. It's easier to take a blindsided breakup less personally when you realize it's about someone lacking tools. The box never came with the missing pieces. Basically, it's not your fault, and when you realize that, the cut is clean. You can move on. Maybe even get to a place where you have empathy for your ex, knowing their pattern of running will catch up with them. Their action, or reaction, is also telling of their character. Simply put, you dodged a bullet.

But a toxic breakup is a different beast. Chances are, if the breakup is toxic, then the relationship was toxic and unhealthy as well. Relationships don't have to be abusive to be toxic and unhealthy. The more unhealthy the relationship, the harder the crash. Because toxic and unhealthy creates a trauma bond: the strong emotional attachment that develops from a cycle of physical and/or emotional trauma followed by positive reinforcement. This cycle creates a powerful and lasting bond. Not just a good glue. A codependent enmeshed glue—a superglue. So instead of an expiration, a breakup is a prying apart. People aren't let go but dragged out of the relationship.

BREAK UP ON PURPOSE

The emotional turmoil and stress from a toxic relationship can persist even after the breakup, impacting your self-esteem, confidence, and even personal safety and making it extremely difficult to focus on your life. You're not just unfollowing someone. You may have to change your address or get a restraining order. Chances are you're going through something traumatic and don't know when it will end.

So after the boundaries are drawn, the safety precautions are put in place, and you've calmed your nervous system, you have to look up for answers. Otherwise, you'll constantly be looking over your shoulder. To believe that this will all work out and that there will be something good at the end of it, you must believe in your own story—the greater-than-you piece.

BREAK-THROUGH WORK

Two things make Susan's particular breakup story important (and different from the others):

1. **Trauma**

   Yes, other breakups can be traumatic, but some, like this one, come with flying chairs. The uncontrolled emotion released by cutting the cord can create panic and a clawing desperation, especially if you and/or your partner struggle with abandonment issues and other wounds. These emotions manifest in reactions, crossed boundaries, and a constant pursuit even when the relationship is over. So the breakup bends instead of cleanly snapping. It lingers.

There's confusion. Emotions are stirring instead of settling. An activated nervous system is on high alert, making it impossible to start healing.

And it takes two to tango. Even if you're not the one slashing tires, the mixture of your two reactions is what creates the explosiveness and probably explains why the relationship didn't work out. You're Coke and he's Mentos: On your own, you're sweet and he's got a perfect subtle fizz that tickles. Mixed together, you're a liquid volcano.

2. **Safety**

People do some crazy shit when they allow their emotions to hijack logic. You've heard the stories, and I'm sure you have a few of your own. These breakups aren't just about healing from a broken heart. They're also about protection. Usually the more explosive the breakup, the more dysfunctional the relationship was, full of enmeshment, codependency, control, loss of self, reactiveness, defensiveness. And the more dysfunctional the relationship was, the fewer tools people have. So when things come to an end in this type of relationship, they usually blow up.

Even if you're the one who ended it, part of you may still not believe or want to believe the relationship is over. It may just be like the last time, because chances are a version of this has happened many times before. Explosive relationships usually go through many rounds before officially ending.

No matter what your friends say, you still believe the relationship could work. So you stay connected in some form, in hopes that your ex will change. You wait. You hit pause on your life and hang on your ex's every move. They're on their best behavior and showing you their "changed" side every chance they get. This creates false hope, keeping you stuck and spinning. Confused. This is when you snap back like a rubber band. Suddenly, you guys are having sex again. You didn't think this would happen. But it did. Like last time. And every fiber of your being is screaming, *No! What are you doing?!*

So you leave again, repeating the cycle of abuse—tension building, incident, reconciliation, and short-lived calm. And every time you do a lap around this cycle, the crazy builds. Until eventually, restraining orders are required.

Pulling yourself away and staying there behind healthy boundaries is more difficult when the relationship was chaotic. This is why learning to "cut the cord" is crucial. Your friends and family won't understand how easy it is for you to snap back and return to a toxic relationship. It's easy because logic will never override the strong pull of relationship dynamics. The more dysfunction, the stronger the pull. Drawing boundaries, processing with a therapist, and staying in touch with supportive friends are all a must.

Cut the Cord

All breakups eventually require healthy space and firm boundaries, but for the toxic chaotic breakup more than any other breakup, establishing space and boundaries is essential. As I mentioned earlier, safety should be your top priority. Unlike in other breakups, your physical safety may be at risk in a toxic breakup. In Susan's story, it wasn't Darren she had to worry about. Wade was the one she had to cut the cord with.

One thing I've learned from many of my own breakups is how hard it is to accept and respect the other person's boundaries. But in looking back, I see what a gift they were. Because I didn't have the courage or tools to draw boundaries myself (cut the cord). Like twenty-six-year-old Wade couldn't. I didn't have the emotional or mental strength to do it. It was someone else exercising their boundary muscle that forced me to exercise mine. If it wasn't for their ability to cut the cord with me, I wouldn't have moved on with my life and started to rebuild. Instead, I would have chased, persisted, and prolonged. I would have been pulled back and forth, wondering if we could go another round, have a second chance. I was swimming in my own emotional riptide and living with false hope. Cutting the cord was a gift, not a curse.

The cord needs to be cut in order for emotions to subside and revelations to surface.

There's a rebirth after every expired relationship. But only if you create the space to have one. That can't happen if your cord is not cut.

Create Distance

Note: If your breakup wasn't toxic or chaotic and you feel safe, it can be followed by a grace period—a reasonable period of love residue. You naturally long for and miss the comfort you had with your ex and in the relationship. As long as the relationship wasn't toxic and abusive and you feel safe, both emotionally and physically, a complete cutoff may not be necessary. Assuming the relationship ended on good terms and you're on the same page, post-breakup sex and a gradual fading may be needed. It's okay and just means you are both human. Besides, the idea of finding someone new you can trust to share your body with may seem light-years away.

So you give yourself a grace period when you go with what you feel in the moment because you're feeling lonely. You don't need to fight it because the intimacy, or lack of, will be the natural cold shower you need. Maybe not the first time, but give it a few goes and both of you will be reminded why things ended. Giving yourself a grace period doesn't mean you have fucked up or that you're stunting each other's growth. After you cut the cord, judging yourself for not being able to draw boundaries fast enough can be just as harmful.

If the relationship has expired, a grace period will not revive it. Unless one of you is not being honest and still wants this. In that case, this is no grace period, but something more like a disgrace period. So both of you really have to be honest with yourselves. The more you wanted to be in the relationship, the faster you need to cut the cord. But if both of you truly don't want to continue, give yourselves grace.

It is very rare that some engagement after the relationship is officially over (relationship residual) re-ignites it and suddenly you both have new insights and revelations and you both genuinely want to rebuild again. Unless breaking up and getting back together is your pattern. In that case, your relationship hasn't truly expired. Breaking up and getting back together *is* the relationship.

For relationships that are truly over and done, a fading tail of emotional and physical attachment is pretty normal. Don't think that just because you had sex with your ex one week after you guys broke up you're back in something you don't want to be in. Be kind to yourself. You and your body may need what you've been used to. A desire to be reminded of that doesn't mean you want to revisit the relationship. It means you need to shed. You need to get it out of your system. Now it's time to draw some healthy boundaries.

All that said, the grace period should last only a couple weeks at most and no longer than one month. A year is not a grace period. That's refusing to let go. The excuses I usually get from my clients who want to stay connected after the grace period include: "I just want to check in to see how he's doing," "I don't want to be with him, but I don't want him out of my life," and "I still care about her." Exactly. That's why you need to be the stronger one. Because maybe he can't right now. That brings me to the other reason why you must cut the cord. You're not just doing it for yourself. You're also doing it for your ex.

What Distance Looks Like in the Day-to-Day

No meetups. No phone calls. No FaceTimes. No texting. No following them on socials. Unfollow them *now*.

Sometimes clients say, *I just want to see how they're doing. I won't engage. I promise.* Well, "seeing how they're doing" is going to bring up a lot of emotions. Will you be able to handle those emotions and not get into your head? What if your ex is dating someone else already? Will you be able to avoid comparing your breakup aftermath with theirs and wondering why you're not further along in moving on? Or what if your ex isn't in a good place? Will you be able to love them from a distance?

Okay, but what if I can honestly say I don't have feelings for them anymore, and it won't set me back if I engage with them? Then ask yourself if engaging with your ex will set *their* healing journey back. If so, you must stay away for their sake. Not for yours.

Cut the cord as if your life depends on it. Because it does—the chance of rebuilding your life depends on it. Yes, you technically may still have a life. You still go to the gym. You still have your friends. You still love Korean barbecue. An expired relationship may not strip you of all this. But here's what happens. Your inner life takes a blow. People put more thought and energy into doing life with someone than they realize, even when nothing is wrong with the relationship. This is just what normal doing life with someone looks like.

Think about it. From the time you wake up to when your head hits the pillow at night, how many thoughts and mini-conversations do you have with yourself about your partner and your relationship? You think about what you want him to change and what you can do to get him to do that. About what to bring home for dinner, or what new restaurants to try. About when you should finally just give him direction because he goes down on you like you're not even there. About the Netflix to-watch list that never gets revised because you're both so indecisive and someone needs to start making decisions. About whether you should talk to him about making decisions because he doesn't really and it's directly affecting your life with him and attraction to him. About how you should go about it, because the last time you tried the two of you ended up in couples counseling with a chauvinist pig. About why he hasn't texted you back when you sent him those loving words. It's been over two minutes!

This is what's happening in your head while you're stopped at a red light. Imagine an entire day of these thoughts. Seven days a week. It only stops when you're sleeping. And even then, it's manifesting in dream energy.

All that is now gone.

Or is it? Just because the relationship has ended doesn't mean that the thoughts and energy we put into it end too. At least, not in the beginning of an expired relationship. They just change. Now we're playing back moments, dissecting, analyzing, trying to piece things together. We wonder how he is doing, if he was faithful the entire time, what he's been honest about and what he hasn't, and what our life would look like now if we had swiped left.

Distance pulls the plug in your cognitive distortion bathtub. Over time, the spinning down the drain slows and you can start focusing on the here and now. Not that your ex has to be cut out of your life forever. Many expired relationships turn into beautiful friendships. But for now, cutting the cord is required for healing to begin. For the distinction between what was and what is to take hold. There is no other way.

Many of my clients skip this step, minimizing its importance. They think they can be friends with their ex way too soon. *The relationship didn't end badly. I still love her and want to be a part of her life. It's all good. We're friends now.* Then I ask them, "Can you go on a double date with your ex and truly be happy for her because she is head over heels about her new love?" I always get silence. Followed by a "Well." Then I follow that up with, "What kind of friend would you be then?"

There is no gray area with cutting the cord. Like marriage, you're either married or you're not. You're not *kinda* married. Or married sometimes. You either did or did not make that commitment. There's no going back and forth. No conditions. No "when I feel down and lonely." Remember, this period doesn't have to last forever. But for now, you have to go through it.

I will simplify and make things clearer for you. Once you do what you have to do now, once you cut the cord, you will be able to breathe.

What about mutual friends?

You will need to decide which friends you will stay connected with and which ones you will draw boundaries with. Are you staying friends with them because keeping up contact is a way to get info about your ex? Or a way to indirectly stay connected to your ex? Which friends will support you? What's best for you at this time? Which friends will make what you're going through all about them?

Cutting the cord also means knowing who you should and should not be friends with. You don't have to make these decisions overnight. Trust that as you get stable, check in with yourself, and start to give yourself what you need, you will naturally push away from people who are not good for you and spend more time with people who are.

Safety Note

People are not themselves when their emotions are running high. Breakups can be activating and cause people to do things they wouldn't normally do. A breakup sends some people into a chaotic spiral that keeps them from thinking logically. Feelings trump logic, always. And these strong feelings can lead to dangerous behavior and situations. If your relationship was toxic and you don't feel safe in cutting the cord, process your situation with a therapist, not just your friends. Friends don't have the clinical background to consider all the possibilities. Come up with a plan with your therapist to cut the cord and create distance between yourself and your ex in a safe and healthy way.

As I mentioned already, trauma and safety are what make a toxic and chaotic breakup challenging. So they should be prioritized and addressed first. Your body was traumatized in this relationship, and if your rational mind tries to minimize that trauma, you'll find yourself defaulting to fight-or-flight-or-freeze, like you're used to doing. This puts a lid on the stored trauma. You may think you're okay and can just go about your day, but the trauma is still in your body, and your body feels unsafe.

You won't know that until you start dating again and something in a new relationship feels unsafe, even though you can't see any obvious red flags. This is because your body believes it's happening all over again. It's trying to protect you. This is also a sign that you need to work through, process, and release your trauma so your body, not just your mind, feels safe again. When trauma isn't processed, it lingers. Many believe that unprocessed trauma is stored in the nervous system. These trapped "issues in your tissues" may have detrimental effects on a person's well-being.

There are many ways to release trauma in the body, such as talk therapy, breathwork, the Emotional Freedom Technique (EFT), bodywork, EMDR (eye movement desensitization and reprocessing) therapy, and sound and vibration healing. But I want to give you something you can focus on daily to get started now. Because, let's face it, we say we'll talk to a therapist about our trauma, but do we really? And if we do, do we stick to it? I can tell you, as a therapist, that the answer is no. Most clients who come to see me are one-offs. One session. Maybe two, tops. They are curious, but not committed.

Yes, a full course of therapy can be expensive. I get it. But that's not the only reason we avoid therapy. We also don't see our breakups as trauma with a capital T. It's a lowercase problem, not a priority. So it takes a backseat. We'll get over it, we tell ourselves. It's just a breakup. These feelings will pass. So we continue to overlook and ignore the trauma stored in our bodies. There is an alternative, though, something you can do right now.

Lead with Your Nervous System

We start the morning activated. We go from lying in a puddle of residual spinning thoughts from the night before to a high dive straight into our inbox and our checklist of to-dos—right after a double shot of caffeine to jolt our system, of course. Then, as the day comes into focus, so do our cognitive distortions. We replay the past and worry about the future—reviewing once again all our what-ifs.

This rumination is compounded if there's an expired relationship in the mix. The normal worry of our daily lives plus the thick cloud of thoughts and emotions from a lost love keep our nervous system activated and operating in overdrive. Pedal to the metal. Running on fumes. Add to that the chaos and danger of a toxic breakup and your nervous system is in a riptide that never ebbs.

Going from this unbalanced state of chaos to being grounded, centered, and connected requires a conscious shift of focus. To reconnect with your conscious self, you must lead with your nervous system.

After going through a chaotic and toxic breakup, you need to protect, prevent, and restore. Most people don't check in with their body—and with their nervous system in particular—when making decisions. Generally, we pull from logic, thinking about how we *should* feel, not how we truly feel. If something makes sense, we do it. If it doesn't make sense, we don't.

But sense doesn't always make a safe choice. Its choices don't always line up with our truth and what we need. Instead of doing something we've been programmed to do since childhood because we believe we should, we need to give ourselves what we need to connect and build trust with ourselves and what protects us from putting ourselves in more traumatic situations. We do this by checking in with our body (nervous system) and listening to it and to our feelings.

You need to engage daily in practices of awareness and regulation that tune you in to the sensations in your body. You need to ask yourself where your head is at by practicing calming and grounding techniques like meditating, deep breathing, and journaling. Or, if you're like me, you'll achieve calm by hitting flow states in a long upbeat workout or by hugging canyons on a motorcycle. Do whatever enables you to find your calm, to feel your feet again. Whatever helps you hear the whispering of your heart and your desires and feel the stirring of your soul. Whatever gets you away from your spinning thoughts.

As you take charge of your body, your state of mind, your emotions and thoughts, as you begin to lead with your nervous system, you will create an intentional energy, a vibration that will keep you out of the lower frequencies—shame, guilt, hate, resentment, jealousy, hopelessness, etc. (constriction)—and living in the higher frequences—love, forgiveness, curiosity, creativity, etc. (expansion). You'll start trusting the power of your own being. And your own story.

Before making any decisions, check in with your nervous system and ask what it needs. This is probably something you're not used to doing. Your parents didn't teach you how to do this. You didn't learn it in school. You're used to getting shit done. Doing what it takes, no excuses. Time is wasting. Or not saying no because you don't want to hurt or upset others. It's easier to just take it. Just do it. What's the big deal?

Well, the big deal is that this becomes your default, your baseline, your norm, and you spend most of your life living activated, in subtle fight-or-flight that you file under normal life stress. No, you may not be experiencing debilitating stress, but a leaky faucet can still drown you if you're not aware of the leak.

When you drop into your body and listen to your nervous system as a daily practice, you'll make decisions that stop activating and retraumatizing. Your new norm will become calming, nurturing, and healing decisions. That's when you'll stop drowning and start swimming.

What Does Checking in with Your Body Look Like in the Everyday?

Your friend is moving and wants to know if you can help her this weekend. As you imagine how this will play out, you drop into your body and notice the tension. There's tightness. There's a subtle panic. You explore where it's coming from. You know very well where it's coming from. This is a friend who's high-strung and demanding. Unless she's changed—which you're not wanting to gamble on right now because you're going through the expiration of a relationship—she will make you feel unseen and unappreciated. That will activate the shit out of you, leaving you jittery and annoyed. Then you will convince yourself that it's okay and that this is what friends do. You will carry that in your body. And most likely hit the drive-through on the way home to make yourself feel better (numbing).

Of course, there will be times you don't want to do something, like help a friend move, but you decide to be generous and kind anyway. Although you'll feel tension and resistance, it's not coming from your friend or your relationship with that person or the space that's created. It's just coming from not wanting to do something. That's not a nervous system thing. That's just an "I don't want to do this" thing. And that's okay.

You have to practice checking in with yourself to know where the tension is really coming from. Sometimes you may be wrong. What's important is to put up this new speedbump before making decisions so they won't be kneejerk decisions but thought-out ones. When you do this, you're giving yourself a say. That's something most of us don't know how to do.

Reminder

If you don't give yourself a say in your own decisions, no one else will.

The Almost-Relationship Breakup

Sometimes the most beautiful relationships are the ones that never had a chance to blossom.

—ANONYMOUS

Now let's swing the other way.

What if you're in something that hasn't solidified into a full-blown relationship yet, but one or both of you decide to end it? Is that technically a breakup? Will you experience the emotional roller-coaster of other kinds of breakups? Or will you minimize your feelings and the impact of this almost-relationship because your friends and family think you're overreacting? After all, they say, *you weren't even in it that long.*

People assume that the longer you're in a relationship the harder the breakup is. But the length of the relationship doesn't always determine how difficult the breakup will be. Sometimes the expiration of a longer relationship is easier to

BREAK UP ON PURPOSE

recover from because the relationship died years before—or before you or he or both of you finally mustered up the courage to put it out of its misery. Sometimes shorter relationship breakups are more crippling. The summer romance that could have been pure magic. The unexpected meeting on a plane that turned into a long-distance fling for a few weeks. When Harry met Sally.

Sometimes losing what could have been is more painful than losing what was.

BRETT AND JACQUELYN

"I like the way you spell your name" was Brett's line after taking two and a half hours to finally walk up to her. Brett had just turned forty and was ready to invest in someone, get married, have kids, and be a good dad—something he'd wanted to be since he was a teen. Teaching his daughter how to swing a bat. His son how to dance. This was what he daydreamed about at work while his friends obsessed about getting laid and driving fancy cars. Brett wanted a simple life. A strong partnership and healthy kids. And unlike other men, he felt old at forty. He felt like his window on becoming a father was closing fast.

Jacquelyn was new to the city and knew nobody. Usually, you meet someone in LA because they're a friend of a friend of a friend. Eventually some link to Kevin Bacon, they say. But Jacquelyn with a "y" didn't even know who Kevin Bacon was. Or maybe she did but played dumb.

She smiled and replied, "Fish?"

Brett grabbed a piece of sushi off the platter she was holding, even though he had vowed to never put fish in his mouth again after a food poisoning incident. And as he took a quick bite, trying to hide the five-year-old in him spitting up peas, she asked him something no one had ever asked him before.

"Have you heard of the term 'cum clarity'?" And that was it. He fell. Literally. That question combined with the gag reaction from the salmon in his mouth caused him to step back and trip over a sprinkler head. He landed in a weird way that split his tight slacks straight down his ass.

People covered their mouths, looked away. Everyone stayed poised—except for Jacquelyn, who also nearly fell over from laughing so hard.

And that's how Brett and Jacquelyn met.

From there it was pretty predictable, something we've seen on the big screen. A young Ryan Gosling would play Brett and some new indie film actress with edge would play Jacquelyn. A quick montage capturing the magic moments. Ice cream. Park benches. Laughter. Legs propped up on the back of theater seats as they take in an afternoon movie like teenagers ditching school. One grabbing the other's hand as they walk. Scenes of Brett in his day-to-day world, sporting shirt and tie at a miserable desk job. But he has a lighter step and a half smile on his face. His job sucks less. Traffic doesn't bother him. Not today. Jacquelyn hustling, going to auditions, taking catering jobs, really trying to make LA work for her. Finally, looking at apartments together.

But here's what we don't see in the rom-com.

Awkward sex. Brett seems nervous. He can't get it up. It gets weird. They sit at the edge of the bed, backs turned to each other as they internalize. Brett at work, looking uneasy, checking his phone. No texts. Jacquelyn on the back of a motorcycle with another dude. As they hug the canyons of Malibu, she throws her hands in the air. He grabs her arms and wraps them back around his waist. Jacquelyn and Brett at dinner. Not a lot of talking. Jacquelyn glances at her phone. Brett notices.

"How do you know it's over?" I asked.

Brett had requested I be direct with him ever since he found me from my blog nearly a decade ago. I still remember our first session. He started with, "I hate therapists who just sit there and ask you how you feel. It's so patronizing." He activated the shit out of me. I had anger issues, and I don't do well with men with anger issues. They remind me of myself.

"She's being less and less responsive. I think she's dating this other guy. She posted a pic with them at the beach. I've never felt this way about anyone. I can't stop thinking about her. I know she's way out of my league but . . ."

Brett starts to pull out his phone.

"You already showed me photos of her."

He buries his head in his hands.

"I fucked it up. I fucked it up. I should have just taken the dick pills."

"Brett, you didn't fuck anything up because there's nothing to fuck up. You guys were just dating. There hasn't been any conversation about exclusivity. Dating is a dance."

"She was perfect."

"No one's perfect."

"I loved her."

"You've only known her for three months. You're feeling the rush of dopamine from the collision and thinking about the life you could have had with her. You don't even know what she would be like in a relationship. Actually you do. Her inconsistency and not communicating is telling. That would most likely ripple over."

He glances blankly out the window.

"I can't believe she broke up with me. We had so much in common. Not to mention we both like boy names for girls."

"Brett, it was never a relationship," I remind him.

And that was the beginning of our work. Although he hadn't technically been in a relationship, Brett was still going through the feelings of a breakup. And that's what we processed.

Brett ended up doing a dozen more sessions. It was harder for him to recover from this almost-relationship than it was for some of my clients recovering from long-term marriages. This was evidence that **the length of the relationship doesn't determine the impact of the breakup and the time it takes to heal.** The what-ifs and "what could have beens" feed the fantasy, turning the knife.

When we're in a relationship, it's not just the relationship making us happy. We get joy from envisioning what we could build with this person in the future. The house, the kids, the tree swing. Or the world travel, the like-minded mission-driven company, or whatever it is that we want. The "building toward" has value. There is palpable energy there.

It's a portrait we're painting with hope and anticipation, and one of the reasons why we work so hard to stay in it. We are investing.

And we are willing to look at ourselves and change for the sake of this investment. So when the relationship expires, we lose not only our partner and the relationship but everything we double downed on. That loss is real, even if it's a loss of something that wasn't real. The dream taken from us is another layer of the grieving cake.

So if you find yourself wondering what could have been, it's okay. As long as you don't live there. The things that almost happen to us are just as powerful as the things that actually do, if not more so. The possibility of a future you could have had with this person makes you feel like you lost more than you actually did. And although it never happened, you keep replaying it as if it did. **Because your body doesn't know the difference.**

Your body just feels the loss and the absence. So as you continue to replay what might have been, you sink deeper and deeper into the pain and exaggerate the loss. The feelings are real, and the chemicals they produce lead to emotional highs that can be addictive. You'll find yourself not just reflecting on what almost happened but living there, soaking in what you believe is hope. But it's not hope. It's false hope. A mirage. This is when you can get obsessive and do things you may regret. Because you're steeped in desperation and want what you lost so bad. This desperate desire prevents you from being present—from accepting, healing, and moving on. You are now living in what could have been. Not in what is.

In one session, Brett finally had the revelation that popped his fantasy bubble.

"We never had a chance. Even if she had worked through her fear of commitment and ambivalence and I worked through my insecurity, jealousy, and clinginess. It would just have been a matter of time before the bottom fell out. It was less about her and more about what she represented. She was my ticket to finally having a family. I'm not happy with my life, so *she* would have been my life, and she would have felt claustrophobic—'grabbed,' as you say. I met her when she just needed to laugh and not take life so seriously. I wanted something completely different. We didn't align. I was recess for her, and maybe I mistook that for love. I don't know, but I guess people don't change fast enough for collisions like this to sustain themselves. As you say, the plane had no wings."

WHAT REALLY HAPPENED

Sometimes we meet people and get something from them that we need at that particular time in our lives. That's what makes the attraction powerful—not necessarily the person but what we get from them. Brett was in a life transition. He was lost, had no sense of purpose, and worked for a catering company to be able to pay back student loans and do things on the weekends. Jacquelyn wasn't just a beautiful woman who caught his attention. She represented how he wanted to feel. Spontaneous. Free. Not giving a fuck. That's what he really wanted.

But Jacquelyn was actually horrible in relationships. Inconsistent. Flaky. Not communicative. Instead of being the "wings" that had been missing on the plane, Jacquelyn was Brett's defibrillator, a reminder that he had to find life in his own life instead of waiting for big things to happen. He was dead. She was air. Brett didn't fall in love so much as remember what it felt like to live again. You can't fall in love unless you experience *how* someone loves. It may be attraction, lust, chemistry. But to be in love requires a thorough investigation and a knowing, doing a complete 360 of a person and their capacity. Not just gazing at the poster.

Once Brett realized what had really happened with Jacquelyn, he was able to take the poster down—to ditch the fantasy so it no longer permeated his feelings and thoughts. He not only saw what happened for what it was but was grateful for the short time they spent together. It didn't have to be anything more. It wasn't supposed to be anything more. The almost-relationship, the one that never happened, was the catalyst that made Brett realize he was waiting instead of living. He was just going through the motions, hoping big things would happen instead of going out and building the life he wanted.

Brett decided to foster a dog. He started taking jiujitsu classes. Met a group of other dudes like him. They shared meals and did ice plunges. Nothing big happened in Brett's life. He had a few new friends he rolled with once or twice a week. He still catered on the weekends. But he had new lenses now. He was no longer waiting. He smashed his internal ticking clock and didn't hold his dreams of being a dad so tightly. He decided that, if it was meant to happen, it would happen. He started to find things in his life that brought him joy. Small things. Daily things.

"Have you ever had a Honeycrisp apple? Not like an old bruised one. A fresh, ripe one?" he asked, like a kid who just had candy for the first time.

"Sure, I believe so," I replied.

"I had one the other day and thought, *Holy shit. This fell off a tree?*"

It was moments like this that proved Brett was changing. He was able to find joy in the little things, things he had in his life right at that moment. His happy wasn't tied to or dependent on things he didn't have much control over. Like love. Like kids and family.

BREAK-THROUGH WORK

What's difficult about the almost-relationship is that you never get to see what the relationship would actually be like. You're filling in blanks, creating a fantasy based on chemicals and projection, not on truth. You haven't experienced all the challenges of being in a relationship with the other person. You guys never built anything. You haven't seen the dirty socks on the floor and how the two of you fight. You haven't seen all the work it takes to make this movie. It's purely a highlight reel, but the more your life feels like a sad documentary, the more leverage the almost-relationship will have on you. Because it was your ticket out.

The prescription is to come back to reality. The more

you start building and finding life in your own life, the less weight that ticket will hold. It was never a way out. It was just a way to get on another ride. The unhappier you are with yourself and your life (the less grounded you are), the crazier that ride would have been. Most likely you would have set yourself up for another lopsided or unhealthy love experience that would have had you internalizing and creating false beliefs about yourself.

Of course we can fall for people fast. The feeling of love can happen in a moment. We can see a future with someone just a few dates in. Someone can appear to be perfect during the dating phase. These feelings, even before we learn how they show up in relationships, are real. Hope and disappointment are not illusions.

I've become enraptured by many I've had a strong connection with, only to be crushed when it didn't last—an almost-relationship. And I would get stuck playing it all back, many, many times, alone in bed, wondering what could have been. Dwelling on what would have happened if I'd only done this or that. If she'd only done this or that. Wishing it had worked out. And if it had, envisioning what my life would look like today. These fantasies would keep me in my head and out of life. The more I fed these distorted thoughts, the more empty and lacking my life felt, the unhappier I became, and the more desperate I became. I was stuck and sinking fast in the quicksand of a chasing state instead of an attracting state.

To stop sinking and pull yourself out, you must stop feeding the fantasy and tripping on the future. What you feed grows, so starve what could have been so you can live in what is. Put that energy into feeding your current life, your real life. That is the vine that will pull you out of the quicksand.

Note: Seeking life nectar (joy) and having firm life anchors (positive spaces) help with all breakups. But for the almost-relationship breakup, they are priorities. The prescription for the almost-relationship breakup, since you feel like you lost what could have been, is to reset by finding value in what you currently have.

Seeking Life Nectar

After my divorce, I got a tattoo of a hummingbird on my left bicep as a reminder to seek nectar. I'd spent most of my life hitting pause and waiting for what I thought would make me happy (including the girl) to come my way. And since it never came, I was a miserable fuck. A miserable fuck with crossed fingers and false hope. I was not living. I was waiting. It wasn't until I hit play on my life by getting out of my head, dropping into my body, and practicing living in the here and now that I was able to feel things like gratitude and true hope, tap into flow states and the power of curiosity and radical acceptance, and start to build happiness. I honed my ability to produce positive emotions instead of feeding negative ones.

The good news is that the longer you stay in this state of living on a higher frequency, the more you start attracting instead of chasing. According to Barbara Fredrickson, known for her "broaden-and-build" theory of positive emotions, a foundational concept within positive psychology, "Whereas negative emotional traits such as anxiety and depression predict a local bias consistent with a narrowed attentional focus, positive emotional traits such as subjective well-being and optimism predict a global bias consistent with a broadened attentional focus."

Our emotional state is more than just a transient feeling. It's the lens through which we view the world. In an expanded emotional state, we see things we couldn't see before. New neurons are connecting as we start to rewire our brains. The world opens up, and we value what we have instead of focusing on what we're lacking. **This is how you break through your breakup.**

Make a list of all the things in your life that bring you joy. Small things, big things, it doesn't matter. As long as they're things you have right now and they're not dependent on the phone ringing or on someone else's yes or no. Not things you want or wish for but things you have in your life right now. It could be your daily pour-over coffee or your yoga practice. It could be a Honeycrisp apple.

Now go beyond just acknowledging and listing these things. Focus and expand on them by dropping into your body and absorbing them. Ask yourself what it would look like to stretch them—to turn them into nectar.

Here's how I stretched my current life nectar:

The first sip of my overpriced ($10) pour-over coffee in the morning: It makes my body feel calm and relaxed. *The stretch:* Allowing myself to have more pour-over coffees without feeling guilty because of the price. Seeing good coffee as protein, not sugar.

Making fresh juice with my daughter: This practice makes my body feel alive. *The stretch:* Incorporating more activities like this one instead of just sitting my daughter in front of a screen. Doing life with her instead of babysitting her.

Waking up realizing I hit REM: Having a good night's sleep makes my body feel energized, fresh, invincible. *The stretch:* Making an effort every night to prepare for a good night's sleep. Going to bed early. Reading and meditating. Using gummies and earplugs. Making sleep hygiene a priority.

Staying a night or two at our vacation cabin in Idyllwild or having a staycation in town: Time off makes my body feel deserving, like I've come a long way and earned this. I feel grounded. *The stretch:* Planning more self-staycations, weekends away, and weekday overnight stays. Prescribing myself short vacation sprints, knowing these are not luxuries or indulgences.

Discovering a new restaurant: Finding a new restaurant makes my body feel excited and curious. *The stretch:* Researching and exploring new restaurants. Making an effort to try new places, whether it's a taco stand or a place that requires reservations months in advance. Because it's not about the food—it's about exploring new experiences.

The birth of an idea: Having a new idea makes my body feel alive and excited. *The stretch:* Creating more spaces where I allow myself to have ideas, without judging them. Having fresh new ideas just to have them, not necessarily with any intention of executing them. Because then logic enters with a bat. Giving myself permission to dream big, as an exercise. Like I used to do before I had to pay taxes.

Riding a dirt bike: It makes my body feel free. Connected to that happy, fearless twelve-year-old in the '80s. *The stretch:* Renting a bike until I buy one. Approaching dirt bike riding—a completely different animal from street bikes and my daily motorcycle rides—like I'm learning a new skill. Riding dirt every chance I get. Also snowboarding every chance I get. I rarely do them because both require prep and planning, but both bring me joy. I will make more of an effort to get them into my life, knowing I want to get better at both skills.

'80s music: Music from the '80s takes me back, in a good way. Hearing it, I instantly feel happy, reminded of my teenage body. *The stretch:* Being that guy rolling up to a stoplight on my Harley blasting Madonna's "Holiday." Using '80s music as a time machine to take me back to my wonder years, some of the happiest times of my life.

Daddy dates with my daughter: Time with my daughter makes me feel like my life is about more than just work and romantic love. *The stretch:* Making more of this nectar by doing more activities with my daughter. Getting to know each other by spending honest time together outside of the expectations of our relationship roles.

Giving free couples sessions for my online community: Being of service makes my body feel purposeful and fills my spirit. It reminds me of why I got into this career in the first place. *The stretch:* Offering more free couples sessions. Feeling the butterflies and being grateful for the privilege of hearing other people's stories.

Now it's your turn. What is the current nectar (joy) you have in your life? How does it feel in your body when you experience it? How are you going to stretch it? The more specific you can be the better.

The next time you experience joy in your life, take a second to drop into your body and really feel the experience, as if you're stamping it into the fiber of your being. Notice the hot rich coffee running down your throat. Take in the majestic sunset as you ride toward it on your motorcycle. Feel the experience like it's the first time you've had it. And take it in like it's going to be the last time.

Remember: life nectar is a gateway to more gratitude and hope, the foundational nutrients we need when going through any kind of breakup.

When you feel gratitude, the neural pathways in your brain associated with reward and positive emotions are activated. The release of neurotransmitters like dopamine and serotonin gives you a pleasurable feeling, replacing any feelings of lack with a feeling of abundance. This can strengthen the neural connections related to gratitude, making you more likely to experience it again. Over time this positive reinforcement can lead to increased feelings of well-being, calm, and optimism. In other words, an overall positive out-look on life.

The Hope Circuit and the Fear Circuit are two distinct neural pathways in the brain that are responsible for processing emotions like hope and fear. They cannot fire at the same time, owing to their opposing functions. The Hope Circuit, centered around the amygdala, is associated with positive emotions, goal-oriented behavior, and optimistic outlooks. By contrast, the Fear Circuit, also involving the amygdala, is related to negative emotions, threat detection, and survival instincts. When one circuit is activated, the other is generally suppressed, allowing the brain to focus on the most relevant response to a given situation.

To activate the Hope Circuit in your brain instead of the Fear Circuit, you can try these strategies:

1. Focus on positive outcomes and possibilities rather than dwelling on negative scenarios.
2. Practice gratitude and acknowledge the things you are grateful for in your life.
3. Engage in activities that bring you joy and fulfillment, promoting a positive outlook.
4. Surround yourself with supportive and positive people who lift up your spirits.
5. Set achievable goals and work toward them, creating a sense of progress and hope.
6. Practice mindfulness and meditation to reduce anxiety and increase optimism.

7. Challenge negative thoughts and replace them with more hopeful and empowering ones.

8. Seek inspiration from stories of resilience and success to reinforce hopefulness.

9. Engage in hobbies or activities that give you a sense of purpose and fulfillment.

10. Remember that hope is a skill that can be cultivated, so be patient and kind to yourself in the process.

Life Anchors

Everyone's life anchor is different. What may be a life anchor for your best friend may not be one for you. For example, fitness may not be a life anchor for you like it is for The Rock. Instead, it may be your motorcycle. Your anchor is whatever gives you a foundation to build your days on.

What I love about life anchors is that they don't have to be some big thing like a purpose, a career path, or a life partner. They can be small things, everyday things. Things that don't hang on someone else's yes or no or require the stars to line up. They can be things you give yourself daily. This brings the power back to you. All that's needed for something to be a life anchor are these three qualities:

It connects you to yourself, making you feel alive.

You practice it daily—it's threaded into your life.

It pulls you out of your head and promotes flow states and presence.

BREAK UP ON PURPOSE

We are programmed to believe that building a life means having a successful career and relationship and, for some, raising kids. And yes, these are important life goals and you can have those things. But you need a foundation first. And if you're going through an expired relationship, chances are your foundation has been rocked. Or maybe you never had one because the relationship itself was your foundation. Either way, now is the time to build one.

Write down what your current life anchors are. Meditation? Yoga? Fitness? Ice plunges? Your weekly online life group? Breathwork class? Twelve-step meetings? Therapy? Or maybe quality time with friends? Surfing? Rock climbing? Art?

What might be some new anchors in your life? How will dropping these anchors into your life change your way of being? Will they change your state and raise your frequency? Will they ground you more? How will executing them daily ultimately change your life?

Reminder
Find life in your life. Because nothing else matters. What's real is what you have now, today. Not what you could have.

The Breakup That Never Ends

The definition of insanity is getting back together with the same person over and over again and expecting different results.

—HEATHER HANSON, LMFT

SEAN AND ANDREA

"Alone, every night alone." These lyrics felt all too real for Sean. The closing music blasted through the club speakers as he ran his fingers over the lip of his glass. As a single tear rolled down his cheek, he couldn't believe he had become this cliché: a guy crying in a club.

They met on Tinder. His best friend, Mark, had recently found his girlfriend on the app, and although Sean had his doubts about finding love with a simple swipe right, he really did want love. And Mark wouldn't shut up about it until Sean gave it a shot.

So there he was, lying in bed. The blue light from his screen touching every wall of his four-hundred-square-foot apartment. Left, left, left, right, left. The whole thing felt a little demoralizing. How could you possibly know if you wanted to date someone based on a few pics and a 150-word bio? He wasn't a shallow guy, after all. And then he came across Andrea.

"Message me if you like grammar and independent women."

Sean *did* like grammar and independent women. Plus, it didn't hurt that she was five-eight, had a great smile, and was rocking a dark pixie cut. His absolute weakness. Her profile also said she was "not looking for anything serious," but it was too late. He was in.

Right swipe. Immediate match. He felt the usual rush you get when you hit on someone at a bar and they actually acknowledge you with a returned smile. *She matched with me! She's down! Wait, what if it was an accident? Like she tried to swipe left but it went right. That happens all the time. No, she's into me. I have to break that pattern of defaulting to the negative. Fuck, now I've got to say something clever. There I go again. Say something, you idiot, she's waiting!*

Sean thought about it for a minute and finally sent the fateful text, an expert blend of confidence and creativity that would have wooed any lucky woman looking for love in Los Angeles.

"Heyy."

Andrea was quick with her response. "Hey? That's the best you've got?" Sean couldn't help but be drawn in by her sass.

They started talking through the app, messaging from the moment they woke up to the second their heads hit their pillows. They shared playlists, favorite foods, cheeky snapchats, and tons of banter. In a way, the mystery of the person behind the screen added to the attraction for Sean.

It was ten whole days before Andrea gave him her phone number. He didn't understand why she was so private about her information, but he kind of admired it. And who cared—he was drunk on attraction. They finally made plans to meet up in person at a frozen yogurt shop near Andrea's house.

Sean was nervous as shit. Sweating bullets all over his best date shirt. And Andrea looked just as nervous as him, but even cuter than her pics. It was usually the other way around. They talked for hours. Frozen yogurt turned into dinner, dinner turned into "let's go back to my place," and sitting at Andrea's place turned into talking all night till the sun came up. This was the moment for Sean. The moment he decided he didn't care what he had to do. He wanted to be with her.

"I mean, she played 'New Slang' on her little iPod speaker that first night, for God's sake," he said in a session once.

It was the first time he truly appeared happy.

"I didn't even tell her The Shins are my favorite band," he confessed.

"I'm happy you found someone you're excited about, Sean."

"You know, it's true what you said. If you just keep working on yourself, you'll attract someone on your level."

I never said that. Besides, this was only our second session, so I don't know how much work he'd actually done. But I didn't want to ruin his moment.

"I would take it slow and really get to know her," I advised. "You don't want this to be like the last one."

"Don't worry. It won't. I have a sharp radar."

Sean spent the next few weeks ignoring all the red flags. He had this question he always asked when he was falling for someone. After growing up with a dad who constantly cheated on his mom, Sean was a bit cynical when it came to monogamy. When he started getting close to someone, he would always ask if they had ever cheated. Two things he had learned from asking this question: people weren't usually so forthcoming if they had in fact cheated before, and if they had, that killed the attraction for him.

So when Andrea told him without hesitation that she had cheated on every partner she ever had except one, Sean was shook. The floor dropped. He knew it'd been too good to be true. But instead of flipping to disinclination, his attraction to Andrea got stronger. Her honesty was so unexpected that it distracted him from considering that she might not be faithful to him. He decided this was going to be the moment when he would choose to see the positive instead of the negative.

"I can't believe she just told me straight up. This is what I've been wanting. Total honesty. No hiding."

I couldn't tell if he was being serious or sarcastic.

"Look, I know what you're thinking."

He was serious.

"All the cheating happened when she was younger. She wasn't ready for a real relationship then. But she is now. She's also in therapy," he explained.

I hate when people use "in therapy" as a marker that someone has changed or is changing. Sean himself was "in therapy" but hadn't done any real work yet. We were just getting started. The first few sessions are just exposition, gathering information and data. What happened to the new client and what led them to my room. Sean didn't book with me because he was going through something. He just wanted to make sure he was "good." Seeing a therapist was more like checking a box so he could tell people he was self-aware.

Sean didn't realize it at the time, but he loved knowing everything his girlfriends were thinking and feeling because that made it easier to tailor his own behavior and prevent them from leaving. Ironically, this initial confession of Andrea's cheating trend made Sean feel like he could trust her. But as the weeks went on and there weren't as many confessions following the first one, the mystery started to feel like secrecy. Sean became suspicious.

He also craved the security of defining their relationship. Bringing it up, though, still felt a bit risky. They hadn't had the "so what are we?" conversation. In fact, they hadn't even come close to that conversation, and yet Sean felt certain that was what was missing from this blossoming connection—the promise between them.

There was a spot she would take him to up in the hills,

overlooking the suburbs where she grew up, where they could park and eat shitty drive-through food like they were in college. Now the chili fries sat between them in Andrea's car, growing cold, as they sat in silence, taking in the glittering hive of the city. It was peaceful and calm for Andrea, almost therapeutic. But Sean was losing his mind.

He hated silence. It reminded him too much of when he was in trouble as a kid. He especially hated it now, as he was about to ask Andrea to be his girlfriend. *This is what we need,* he reminded himself silently as he searched for the courage to force the words out. Little did he know that "forcing" would become habitual between him and Andrea.

Let's just say she was less than ecstatic when he asked her to be his girlfriend. In fact, she was appalled by the question. For Sean, the missing piece to their relationship was just tossed out the window. Suddenly they were having a huge fight. Their first fight. They went back and forth for nearly two hours, with Andrea being painfully honest about her lack of desire to make it official and Sean making his case for why she should just agree to be his girlfriend. It was a mess. Andrea ended it right there.

Now Sean had some real work to do in our sessions. He was hurting and needed to process. His mom and dad constantly fought and threatened each other during his wonder years, right in front of him. He never knew if they would be together or not when he came home from school. Even though they never separated, they talked about it openly. He believed that they stayed together because of him. They were never happy, and he blamed himself for that.

After realizing that his need to define their relationship was tied to his upbringing and the anxiety of not knowing if his parents were together or not, Sean reached out to Andrea for another go. He promised he didn't need a label anymore. They could just casually date and "go with the flow." After she declined, he said he couldn't let go of the attraction he felt for her, and that "connections like this don't come around that often."

Sean was persistent. He did not give up. Eventually, Andrea gave in. In a bittersweet win for Sean, they officially entered round two. But now things flipped. Andrea was the one who wanted to define the relationship. In her mind, they needed to officially be boyfriend and girlfriend because this was the relationship that would break her pattern of cheating. So they became boyfriend and girlfriend. And things looked good from the outside—but didn't feel as good for Sean as he thought they would. Officially being Andrea's boyfriend didn't make him feel secure but only added pressure.

Sean resorted to finding new reasons to feel like Andrea was going to leave him. He wanted to spend every night together, but Andrea wanted her own space. He wanted to bring her to his family functions, but she wanted to meet up with him after. He posted her on his social media often. But she was "just a private person" and didn't feel comfortable posting him to hers.

After eight months of this, the focus gradually shifted from building their connection to building their relationship. This is an essential differentiation. Sean was no longer thinking about what had initially drawn him to Andrea. Her smile, her style, her sense of humor. In fact, he lost all sight of what he actually wanted. It was almost like a game to Sean. He was the gatekeeper and Andrea was a prize to be won. Sean was certain that he was constantly at risk of someone stealing Andrea from him. Or worse, Andrea simply leaving him.

It also didn't help that Andrea worked as a stripper. She quite literally made her living by entrancing other people, a job that made him feel insecure. It didn't feel like a problem to Sean at first. He actually liked that she was so confident and in touch with her body. He also liked the feeling he got knowing that everybody wanted her but he was the only one who had her. Now that he was her "boyfriend," he felt he had a right to ask her questions, to know exactly where she was and who she was with at all times.

He also started noticing things he hadn't noticed or cared about when they weren't calling themselves boyfriend and girlfriend. When she slept over, her phone would vibrate at odd hours of the night. She would set her phone face down after looking at it, so the notifications weren't visible. She even flaked on a few plans at the last minute and couldn't come up with reasons that made sense. Worst of all, when he brought this up with her, she would brush it off or make him feel like he was crazy.

Was he just a jealous and possessive boyfriend? Or was she deflecting and hiding something from him? These questions plagued him relentlessly. He was beginning to understand why people went through their partner's phone. He never wanted to be that person, but at a certain point he couldn't help himself and his curiosity got the best of him.

Sean already knew Andrea's phone password, which made it easy to go through her phone when she fell asleep. It's a still rush, waiting for someone you love to fall asleep next to you so that you can sneak past them and invade their privacy. In the name of love. He slipped out of the bed without making a sound. *I'm doing this for us,* he said to himself, starting to feel a little guilty. But then he saw the messages.

Not just one, not just two, but four different men that she had been messaging. His worst fear was realized. He woke up Andrea and began packing her things without explanation. He wanted her out of his apartment.

"What's going on?" she said. But she knew. She saw her phone lying on the carpet next to the bed, not where she left it, and started word-vomiting apologies. Sean just carried on packing her things. He could never be with someone who cheated on him. That was the most basic boundary in his eyes. Andrea begged him to let her explain as he rushed her out the door, but he didn't want to hear it. He just wanted her gone so he could process what he had found on her phone.

She left reluctantly, and her guilt over hurting Sean seemed genuine, which made him question whether he should have rushed her out. He wasn't even sure if they had to end. This was the girl he said he'd do anything to be with. The quick-witted girl with the pixie cut he had finally convinced to be with him after weeks of trying to persuade her. Maybe he was being unreasonable. Cue little red devil on his shoulder.

"No way, bro. She lied to us. Screw that broad," the devil fussed. Meanwhile, on Sean's opposite shoulder, the angel bartered with him: "She's human, just like us. We should hear her out."

Sean was lost. His ability to decipher which of his needs were reasonable and which were "needy" went completely out the window when he thought about Andrea. He pictured her crying on her way home. He fantasized about her begging him to take her back, unapologetically wanting him. He hadn't felt that before. She had always seemed indifferent about their relationship status. It gave him a strange sense of security to think that this incident could be what changed her mind. Made her ready to really commit. Fuck boundaries. Fuck his needs. If Andrea was ready to really commit, Sean would be willing to overlook this little cheating thing.

He went to bed that night still hurt, but hopeful. He put the devil and angel to bed for the time being and made a mental note to text Andrea in the morning.

When he woke up the next day, it was like he'd been injected with a shot of confidence. He felt secure, he felt powerful, and he was certain there would be a storm of texts from Andrea awaiting him when he checked his phone. Boy, was he wrong. He picked up his phone. No notifications. *Weird*, he thought. *Maybe she's feeling too guilty still.* His confidence rapidly began to deflate. He decided to just give her a call. The phone rang . . . and rang . . . and rang. He was starting to think she wasn't going to pick up, but on the fifth ring she finally answered.

"Sean?" She had that raspy morning voice he had come to know and love so much. "I thought you said you never wanted to talk to me again," she said in a surprisingly snarky tone for someone who had just been caught cheating. Sean didn't really know what to say, so he just spoke his mind and asked, "Can I see you?" She paused for a second before saying, "I don't think that's a good idea."

She explained how sorry she was for hurting him, but also how relieved she was that this was over. She never cheated on him. Those messages were from her guy friends. But she was also reminded why she never wanted a relationship in the first place. She didn't want to feel grabbed and controlled.

But Sean wasn't taking no for an answer. Back and forth they went, in an oddly familiar fashion. It felt like they were in their early days again. Andrea seeming painfully disinterested and Sean desperately trying to reel her in. He somehow found himself in the position of begging Andrea to give them another shot. "We can make this work," he said.

Andrea must have sensed that nothing she had said so far was getting through to him, so finally she said, "I didn't even want to be in a relationship in the first place. You just never believed me when I told you that." This conversation was going very differently than Sean had expected. They lingered in silence for a beat, and then she said, "I have to go to work. I can't deal with this shit right now," and hung up the phone. No chance of rebuttal, of more persuading. It was done for real.

Sean tried to numb the devastation of rejection by hanging out in clubs, strip clubs. Every song reminded him of her. Who, by the way, decided that all the pop songs need to be about breakups? The ones that aren't about breakups are about love, and the majority of those are actually just crooning about glorified pursuer-withdrawer dynamics.

But back to poor, sad Sean. He did his time crying in the strip club, making dancers feel weird. Eventually, he'd be asked to leave. He sulked at home and hugged the ice cream tub extra tight. Luckily for him, the devastation he thought would last forever was no match for time.

After a few days had gone by, he started to feel some relief. Now that he wasn't constantly trying to prove himself worthy of commitment, he had a ton of time to reconnect with himself. And it seemed like the more he reconnected with himself, through sitting with his feelings, journaling, and processing with me, the clearer his relationship with Andrea became. He started to wonder if it was Andrea he was in love with or the idea of her.

"Or maybe it was more about getting her to put her clothes back on," he said out of the blue during one session.

"So you think this was more about you being a hero?"

"Maybe."

"Was there something about not being able to fix your parents' relationship that fueled your desire to fix this one?"

He didn't respond. But I saw in his eyes that the answer was an unequivocal yes.

Six months later, Sean ran into Andrea at a gas station. She looked different. She'd grown her hair out and no longer had the pixie cut. She'd gained a little weight. The first thing she said was that she quit dancing.

They decided to have coffee and catch up. She hadn't dated anyone since Sean. She said she missed him and realized she'd been running from him. Like she always did. The coffee turned into dinner and drinks and a night of passion. Andrea told Sean she thought that was the first time she ever "made love." It was an indirect way of saying she had changed, that she was growing.

By this time, Sean had stopped seeing me. He felt he was good. But he scheduled an "emergency" session to tell me that he ran into Andrea and it ended up at his place. He said they were thinking about giving the relationship another shot.

I asked him the question I ask all my clients who want to try again: "What would be different this time?"

Sean didn't have any answers.

I don't know if they ended up getting back together, but if they did, chances are it was followed by another expiration. I don't know about Andrea, but Sean hadn't experienced enough internal change. He was just starting to work through his wounds.

It's not just time that breaks patterns. People have to change from the inside out. Sean was definitely on his way, but he hadn't come out the other side yet. Many believe that things will be different simply because they have started the process of change and growth, but then they snap back. There has to have been enough time to develop new wiring and lenses, and that doesn't happen in a matter of weeks. Also, if the other person hasn't changed, chances are the two of them will just be tracing old patterns. *Both* of them must show up as different people for the relationship to have a chance. And this is very rare. That's why the breakup that never ends is so common.

WHAT REALLY HAPPENED

Sean wasn't interested in saving Andrea, like most men who had dated her had tried to do. He wanted to save the relationship because it was tied to his self-blame for not being able to save his parents' marriage. But Sean's parents' marriage had ended way before they parted. It was a flat soda breakup. For years they were sleeping in separate rooms. Displaying no affection. Sean felt that energy. Kids know. And he blamed himself for it. He made it his task to save their relationship, but that was impossible for him to do.

Andrea didn't break up with Sean because he went through her phone, because of his invasion of her privacy. After all, she'd been dating nothing but controlling, possessive boyfriends. She was used to it. Yes, she wanted someone new and different. But she felt that this relationship could be the one that broke her pattern of infidelity and she wasn't ready for that. She didn't break up with Sean because he was bad for her. She broke up with him because he was good for her.

BREAK-THROUGH WORK

Simply put, the challenge with the breakup that never ends is to break the pattern of getting back together. That behavior pattern itself can be an addiction, very similar to the intermittent rush of "I love you, get away" found in trauma bonds. This unhealthy cycle can create its own momentum and gravitational pull. The false calm of a reunion can feel like a safe tree as we give ourselves excuses for going back.

There are going to be days when you feel like you got this and days when you're curled up in the shower sobbing uncontrollably because you miss his scent. Or the way her top lip curls when she smiles. Remember, recovery from this type of breakup is cumulative. What you feel right now is temporary. Know that your feelings are not facts. Just because you feel something doesn't make it truth that you should act on. Remember, it will get easier. You will notice the sky again. Not because it's falling but because you can finally connect with the wisdom and hope lining those dark clouds. Know that.

If you feel like you're getting sucked back in, start by asking yourself the question I asked Sean: "What's going to be different this time?"

You have to know and understand that if there hasn't been internal growth and change for both parties—not just acquiring new tools but also showing up differently in the relationship—everything that didn't work before is still there. The attraction may be strong, but that doesn't mean it's healthy, and besides, attraction alone isn't enough to build a healthy, sustainable relationship. Usually breakups that go through many rounds are short-lived relationships. They are sprints, not marathons. Many break up when the honeymoon phase fades and reality hits, hard. When the two partners realize how different they are. Or how reactive their fights are. Or they see their inability to own.

So one of them ends it, or sometimes both of them. Then, after some time has passed, they get lonely, watch all the highlight reels, and consider giving it another chance. Maybe things will be different this time. They may see some change, and their intentions may be honest, but the dynamic that broke the relationship is still there and will break it again. So they go back to their corners. Focus on their own lives. Maybe even date others. And the longing starts again. They minimize. Or forget. And suddenly, they're back in the ring again.

Ask yourself why it didn't work. Write it down. See it on paper. What would it take to change what didn't work? What kind of inner transformation would have to happen? How far are you and your ex from that? Are your values and goals unaligned? What wounds must be healed? What spaces must be created? How can conflict be better resolved?

Here are some common reasons why it didn't work the first time.

The two partners outgrew each other. (One of them started their self-actualization journey and the other didn't.)
Their definitions of love didn't align anymore.
Trust was broken (infidelity).

When it was good, it was great. But when it was bad, it
   was really bad. (It got toxic.)
They didn't know how to resolve conflict in a healthy way.
They were at different stages in their lives. (For example,
   one wanted marriage and family while the other wanted
   to focus on career and travel.)
One of them, in recovery, fell off the wagon.

Old Patterns Must Break to Break Through

Yes, you've always been attracted to tall musicians or men
with muscle. You know you like ambition, humor, and al-
mond eyes. But those are preferences, not patterns. By patterns, I mean the type of person you've been drawn to. What
type of person do you always end up with? Why does this
happen? What is the underlying tug you feel?

Do you find yourself with fixer-uppers—people with po-
tential who, with your involvement in their life, could really
do some big things? Being with this type of person gives
you a cape, a sense of purpose and possibly value. Do you
go for those who are emotionally unavailable? Maybe it's
easier to love this type of person because you don't have to
truly show yourself. Or maybe it's just what you're used to.
Your upbringing makes them smell familiar. You don't know
anything else.

Maybe you're drawn to those who sink into obsessions.
These mad scientists are exciting and filled with passion
because they allow themselves to fall deeply into whatever they do or whomever they love. You envy them that,

because you are not wired that way. But they can also be narrow-minded and prone to controlling borders. Maybe they're not full-fledged addicts, but their addiction always rides shotgun. Maybe their dependency on you is what you're attracted to.

Breaking up with this type can default you to victim mode—the most powerless state. They did something to you. They broke their promise. They left you. They betrayed you. Hard stop. On life. But if you can understand why you're attracted to this type, then you can bring it back to you—where the power always lives. Understanding yourself better is gold. It's the traction you need to push yourself forward so your life keeps going and you continue growing.

Review your past relationships and write down what you see as the common thread in your attraction to others. Are there any patterns in what makes you gravitate toward someone? Not what's on their outside. I'm not referring to types. What's the current running underneath? What is the draw and why is it there? Is it healthy or unhealthy? If it has only led to unhealthy relationships, what would breaking this pattern look like for you? Obviously, not getting back together with your ex. But what else? Go deeper. What needs to be explored and healed within for you to show up differently? What resistance would need to be worked through to give yourself a new love experience? Would you need to toss your "types" and focus on different things? Would you need to explore the parts of yourself that attract a certain type of unhealthy person?

Once your patterns are broken, giving your self and your body a new love experience is what will recondition it so you don't snap back into unhealthy patterns.

Reminder

Growth is all about breaking patterns. It requires an honest look at self, ownership, and a lot of reps. You don't have to live in what was anymore.

The D Word—Divorce

Divorce happens now not because we are unhappy,
but because we could be happier.

—ESTHER PEREL

Divorce doesn't check all the boxes as a type of breakup, but for our purposes here we'll use that label. Ideally, this type of breakup should be called a "conscious uncoupling" that shows respect for the love and its changes and that dissolves the relationship with integrity and love. Ideally, the two exes will actually grow after the expiration of their relationship. Because marriage can be one of the most significant and challenging life changes anyone can go through.

Unfortunately, an amicable marital breakup is not the norm. So chances are, if you're going through a divorce, the term "conscious uncoupling" may only make you feel frustrated and alone. Because in your case that's not what's happening. If so, you're going through what most of us experience during a divorce. A lack of love and respect. Reactions from hurt feelings. A chess game. Children used as pawns. You may also be struggling with the societal stigma, shame, and judgment. And I don't want to minimize that. So let's just call the final type of breakup "the D word."

Note: According to the American Psychological Association, approximately 50 percent of first marriages end in divorce. The rate for second marriages is even higher, with 60 to 67 percent of them breaking up.

LAUREN AND SCOTT

Lauren wondered if she'd willed it to happen. Or had her intuition just been that on point? She flashed back to the heated conversation they'd had months ago, when Lauren accused Scott of being inappropriate with the receptionist, Catherine, at his medical clinic. "You're just asking to get MeToo-ed!" she'd yelled, hoping that angle would keep him from flirting with his employee. Lauren knew she was attractive herself, but at almost forty-four, she also knew she couldn't compete with a twenty-six-year-old.

Scott and Lauren's marriage had been challenging for the last few years, especially after they had a daughter. They had never wanted children. They wanted to work remotely, travel, and experience different cultures. They wanted to never have to schedule sex and to be that exciting aunt or uncle you want to be like when you grow up.

But their lives had been far from that for years. Lauren had accidentally gotten pregnant and had a miscarriage. Hearing a real heartbeat shifted something in both of them.

Scott went into a mild depression after they lost the baby. But Lauren felt nothing but anger. She was mad at her body for failing her and became determined to have a baby. Scott wasn't sure, but he wanted Lauren to be happy. Lauren got pregnant shortly after, and they had a beautiful girl they named Eva. Now they were anchored to domestic life as they learned to be parents, coped with being sleep deprived, and woke up in separate rooms with compounding resentment from the day before.

It was during this time that Scott hired Catherine and Lauren began to notice a shift in his behavior. At first, she liked this more energetic version of her husband. He got back to getting outside and rock climbing, and he seemed to have a twinkle in his eye again. But Lauren's initial intrigue was replaced with dread after she attended Scott's holiday party and was introduced to Catherine. She was stunning, with long, loose brown curls that framed her porcelain doll–like face. Deeply intuitive, Lauren could feel Scott's guilt as she shook Catherine's hand. It was two weeks later that she tried the "MeToo" angle to scare him into resisting temptation, and two months later that he told her, over their Thursday takeout Thai, that he wanted a divorce.

She remembered being fixated on the mostly finished pad thai sitting in the middle of the table. How the hell had he been able to sit across from her and ask her about her day, shoveling noodles into his mouth, while knowing he was going to drop this bomb? "Are you . . . are you fucking kidding me?" she stammered.

"Don't worry," he said calmly. "You can keep the house."

"What about our daughter?!" she screamed.

"I'm not going anywhere. I'll still be her father," he explained.

The next few months were a blur. Lauren's mom and best friend took turns on "suicide watch" and took care of Eva during some of Lauren's darkest moments. Lauren felt shattered, abandoned, so so angry, and guilty for not being fully present for Eva. She felt like a shitty mom and blamed it on Scott. She frequently flashed back to their wedding day and every anniversary thereafter, when he looked into her eyes and said, "I've been searching my whole life for you." Now they had a family and a home in the middle of being remodeled. "How could he do this to us?" How could he throw away everything they'd built for some girl twenty years his junior? After all they'd been through together?

The truth was, it wasn't even about the new girl. There was no infidelity. No flirting. Scott wasn't interested in Catherine. He had been unhappy in his marriage before he even hired her. They had problems that Lauren had minimized, swept under the rug, didn't want to face. They were drifting.

She admitted that Scott tried to get her into couples therapy, but she was already in therapy (with me) and thought that was enough. Maybe she also thought that having a baby would fix any problems in the marriage. When you have a baby, you have other priorities, she thought. Your "problems" aren't really problems because there are more important things at hand. It's not about you anymore. Also, a baby can bring people closer. Suddenly you have a family.

But that idea backfired. Having a baby took a crowbar to their marriage. Scott and Lauren were sleep deprived, had no time for themselves, and were always in a panic state. They drifted even further apart. They weren't good at being parents. A baby just added more pressure and stripped them of sleep. It tested their marriage, and their marriage broke. A divorce wasn't what Lauren wanted, but Scott didn't see any other way out. He didn't think the marriage was fixable.

Lauren also had to grieve her "secondary losses." If the primary loss was Scott, the secondary losses were everything that came with him: Scott's loving family, their mutual friends, their dual income, their Airbnb rental—the lifestyle they had.

Lauren couldn't focus or even leave her bed some days, so her mom moved in with her to take care of Eva. Lauren took a leave from the hair salon where she worked. She just couldn't fake it with her clients, and she felt apathetic about everything. But she eventually realized that the lack of structure and connection in her life was making her more depressed, and after six weeks she returned to work. She didn't wear mascara again for six months, though, because every conversation seemed to trigger tears. It didn't matter if her client was talking about a show they'd seen recently or a tropical vacation they'd just returned from—everything reminded Lauren that she was in her forties and starting over again.

But something shifted around the nine-month mark. By

then, Lauren was thoroughly enjoying her Sundays. She would take her daughter on long walks, meet girlfriends for brunch, and spend the afternoon painting in Scott's former office, which she'd now turned into an art studio. When she and Scott first got together, Lauren stopped painting. She focused her evenings and weekends on him—on taking care of his needs. Lauren's parents had been very traditional, and she believed that she needed to spend her after-work time cooking, cleaning, and spending time with Scott. But in giving up painting and deprioritizing her friends, she'd unknowingly deprioritized herself in the process. And then, even with all of those sacrifices, he'd still discarded her like an old pair of shoes.

One Sunday in August, Lauren realized not only that she actually enjoyed her own company but that she'd really missed herself for the last seven years. She'd been so focused on running toward the picket fence that she hadn't asked herself what made her happy. She'd been so focused on "loving" Scott that she hadn't loved herself. Reflecting back, Lauren realized that she'd been in relationships for most of her life, and that most of her energy and love had gone into her partner, not herself. Vowing to spend the next year channeling all her love inward, she decided that, when she was ready to date, she would never "lose herself" in a relationship again.

Two years later, Lauren was still single—and happy. She had bad days like everyone else. But overall, she was a happier person than she'd been while married, with more clarity and understanding of self.

In looking back with clearer lenses, she saw that her marriage had died years before Scott said he wanted a divorce, that she had just been hanging on because she thought that was what you did. She thought that was what love looked like. You didn't leave because things got hard. You stayed because you promised you would. And you adjusted. Learned to love. Again, and again. Even after it was broken. Two years later, she had realized she was sold a lie. People can change, and marriages can die. And divorce doesn't have to mean you failed. It can mean you're finally being honest with yourself. Not every relationship is fixable.

Of course, sometimes she missed the fancy vacations and galas, but she realized that she got more from connecting to herself—whether painting or going for a long walk—than she ever did at fancy events. She had reconnected with her girlfriends, two of whom were also divorced. One of them helped cohost Lauren's first art show. She couldn't believe she sold four pieces on the spot!

She was open to dating, but her main priority was herself and her daughter. Scott took Eva every other weekend. Lauren and Scott now had a solid friendship—the best relationship they'd ever had, and they were great parents. Lauren believed that, if not for the divorce, she would never have truly found herself, with impacts on her ability to be a good mother. She had needed to be single so she could rebuild an authentic life.

"Being single can actually be quite wonderful when you're not freshly heartbroken and thinking the sky is falling. I've learned that the key variable is fostering a strong relationship to the self. Although things may appear the same, everything changes."

WHAT REALLY HAPPENED—DIVORCE IS THE BEGINNING, NOT THE END

I chose this story because it illustrates so well that divorce doesn't have to mean the end. It can actually be the beginning. Our world defines "divorce" as failure and stamps "defective" on the foreheads of those of us who have been through it. It's no wonder so many stay in dead marriages that are no longer fixable or honest for them. We don't want to be used goods, an open box model. We don't want people to think we're salvaged. We don't want to suffer the stigma of divorce. We have failed. We weren't enough. We're defective, old, unlovable.

When people find out you're divorced, they instantly express sympathy. As if someone died. You carry a noticeable love stain, a salvaged title. The idea of finding someone else and starting all over again can seem daunting and a lifetime away. And everything is amplified for single parents. More apologies, rumors, and louder clocks. It feels like the end of the world. I get it. I was there. As were many of my clients.

The truth is, we didn't fail. The truth is, people change and drift and no longer want the same things. The truth is, we get married young without tools and realize only later how difficult married life can be. The truth is, we say yes because of a ticking clock, and we stay because our left brain tells us to. The truth is, we forget to work on our marriage because we have kids to raise and bills to pay. The truth is, life happens.

But one day you wake up and realize two things.

You don't like your life. But more importantly, you don't like yourself.

I would not be who I am today if it wasn't for my divorce. It chopped me down at the knees, but it also gave me new legs. Stronger legs. Rebuilding myself repositioned me, gave me the perspective, mindset, and tools I needed to run toward my true north. After the shock and heartbreak, after wiping tears from my eyes on many Friday nights, wishing I could have saved the marriage and wondering what was wrong with me because I couldn't, I finally saw that there had been nothing to save. My marriage was meant to be a catalyst to my inner journey.

If my marriage had never expired, there would have been no reason for me to look inward and do some real work on myself. And who the hell wants to take an honest look at himself and take ownership of his shortcomings and the unfulfilling life he has made for himself? It's so much easier to hide inside a marriage. To pretend to be oblivious and numb. I would have been like my parents, sleeping in separate rooms and together only because of shoulds and fear of being alone.

Now, over a decade later, I look back with a fresh layer of empathy for myself and for my ex-wife. I see what I couldn't see when I was in it: why the plane went down. And I can see my part in crashing the plane. I remember now that when she said, "I'm not happy," on one of our nightly walks, I casually dismissed that comment as if she were just noting the weather. I see how not present and out of tune I was.

There were no monsters in our marriage. Only desperation, panic, and a line drawn in the sand for the first time with shaky hands—hers. This wasn't about her not loving me. It was about her loving herself. Maybe for the first time. And about me not having a sense of self or the ability to create a safe space or build something healthy. What happened wasn't a car crash. It was simply young love. Two kids doing the best they could. The sky didn't fall. It never opened.

Until we divorced.

I'm not pro-divorce. I think we should do everything we can to fix a marriage, including individual and couples therapy. I actually believe that most people give up on their marriage too soon. But I *am* in favor of peeling labels off anyone who is divorced. Divorce doesn't have to be a tragic event that stains your story. Divorce can be a break between the acts that propels your story forward. It can be the beginning of you. Not the end.

If you're going through a divorce, you must scrap the stigma. You must drop the baton that was passed down from your parents. From their parents. And from churches. **The ending of a marriage is not failure.** For most people who divorce, it is an awakening. Failure is staying in something that's toxic, unfulfilling, and dishonest. Divorce takes courage, but it can imbue your life with freedom, realignment, and a new sense of worth. Divorce is a rite of passage. It's a form of the hero's journey, with a better you waiting at the end. Remind people around you to stop saying "I'm so sorry" when they find out you're going through a divorce. Instead, tell them congratulations are in order.

BREAK-THROUGH WORK

Now let's get to the work. What makes divorce different from the other breakups is the intricacy and enmeshment of the marital relationship. It is a wire-netted fence. Families have been legally linked, children are permanently tied to both parents, and as with Scott and Lauren, secondary losses are suffered. A house, pets, children, friends, property, and even businesses can be lost. Unlike other breakups, which usually leave your world unchanged, a divorce can crumble everything. Your day-to-day can change drastically. Divorce is a type of breakup that may require a complete life redo. It's not just a transition. It's also a deconstruction of your identity. You're not just letting go of the person you loved. You are letting go of who you were.

But out of this collapse can come a rebirth. You can truly change all areas of your life, not just one part of your life, and you can change from the inside out. That's the game changer. You're starting over, but this time you're making decisions from unfiltered truth.

It's said that if you just pivot a few millimeters when swinging a golf club, over time the ball will end up in a completely different place. It's the same when you make decisions that are not swayed by society, family, friends, blueprints from previous generations, or who you used to be, but rather from an honest place, from who you are today. Yes, starting over after a divorce can be terrifying and overwhelming. You don't know where to start or what life after divorce even looks like. You've never done this. The muscles you need to go forward are weak. Start by giving your self no choice.

First, a Promise to Yourself

I will help you with structure and mindset, what has worked for me and my clients. I will give you areas to focus on and steps to take that will help you start building a new life. But first, you must not give yourself a choice. Let me explain.

After my divorce, I was forced to find a new place, make new friends, reevaluate my career, look inward, and explore internal barriers, beliefs, and childhood wounds. I was forced to reflect, reassess, and start the process of understanding myself and what I wanted out of this life. No, no one put a gun to my head. By "forced" I mean that the other choice was to see myself as a victim, to fall into a depression, be unhappy and angry, and just go through the motions of life as a miserable fuck—which is what I was for all of my twenties and early thirties. Now, at thirty-five, I was not willing to reverse and go back to living that way, which had actually contributed to the crumbling of my marriage. There was only one gear for me—forward.

When things got hard, confusing, lonely, discouraging, I reminded myself that I'd burned the boats. This was the island I would live or die on. It was that binary for me. Life or death. But that view of what it all meant was also completely true. Either I would die a slow internal death or I would be reborn.

So I made a single promise to myself:

**No matter what happens,
I will never go back to who I used to be.**

This was my mantra. It was what I saw every time I looked up. It's what I thought about when I was on my last round of burpees during a hard workout and wanted to quit. When I stood outside my therapist's office, wondering if I should go in. I thought about it every time I felt sorry for myself, or didn't want to get out of bed, or just wanted to numb, to hide, to run away. Every time I wanted to quit something I knew was good for me, I went back to my promise to self.

This promise to myself gave me tremendous leverage because it was based on emotion, not logic, and it was tied to my story. Our emotions will always hold more sway than logic. Our emotions are the elephant, and our reasoning minds are the little riders on top of it. At the end of the day, the elephant is going to go where it's going to go. Nothing will give you more power than your story and the emotions tied to it.

Remember, divorce, more than any other breakup, isn't just about getting over someone. It's your stake in the ground, your break between the acts of your life. *I'm done. That's it.*

I'm building something new. For myself, not for others. I want more. I want different. No more going through the motions. No more muting myself. No more walking on eggshells and doing life around people. I want to explore new love in all my relationships, including the one with myself. I want to explore new work and passions, sex and creativity, things I never had time for or didn't think I deserved. I want to explore a brand-new life. Fearlessly, with gratitude, forgiveness, courage, and dignity. Without comparisons, shoulds, pressing timelines, patriarchal maps. No more living in the past. No more fear of the future. I want now. To know in this moment who I am and what moves me. I want to live like I'm dying. Because for most of my life I haven't done that, and it almost killed me.

Sounds great. But also overwhelming. Where do you start?

Let's take a breath, pull back, and start with what I call a "life audit."

Audit (Realign) Your Life

When was the last time you did a complete audit of your life? You may have examined parts of your life. But when have you taken a big step back and examined your life in its entirety?

Chances are, the answer is never. Because who does that? Relationships actually cause us to *not* look at our lives. We are too busy making someone else happy. Or finding our own happiness in someone else.

It's all too easy to live in a bubble in a marriage, even a healthy one. In a slow drip over time, you can lose the life you once had and liked before you met the person who is now your ex. And just because you were "busy" in your marriage doesn't mean you had a life. You may have spent most of your days getting the kids to school and doing all the domestic work that needed to be done. Maybe sitting through Zoom meetings in a dead-end career that didn't fulfill you, sitting there dressed from the waist up and looking like you cared. Shopping for groceries, getting chores done, attending parent-teacher meetings, watching your kid's soccer games. Not to mention all the emotional energy you spent on trying to save or fix the marriage. Personal therapy, couples counseling, and forced date nights that made you guys feel like at least you were doing your "homework."

Most of this is now gone. Yes, you still may have responsibilities, but except for your kids if you have them, you are not accountable to someone else. And yes, your job may still suck, but chances are you are contemplating a new career path since so much else is changing in your life. You realize this is a good time to wipe the slate clean. Simply put, you have a lot more time and energy now. What you do with it is the question.

I wanted to see where most people would start. So I asked on social media, "If you were to do a life audit, where would you start?"

Here's what people said.

Friends
Looking into the reasons I entered my last long-term
  relationship.

My low self-esteem. I would tend more to that part of my
    life by giving it the love it deserves.

Health routine

My self-worth

Self-value. Not attaching it to my relationship status.

I need hobbies to work on.

Finding out what my professional calling is

Health, nutrition, and career change

Eliminating toxic people

Setting boundaries

How to relax

Work-life balance

Self-honesty

Carrying responsibilities that don't belong to me

My constant anxiety

Sense of worth. Partner became abusive in last relationship
    after I disclosed affair.

How I spend my personal energy

Anxious attachment, ruminating, obsessive, intrusive
    thoughts when I'm in a relationship

My abandonment issues

My finances

Plug the Leaks

First, let's start wide, keeping it simple. That's where po-
tency lives. I find that the simpler concepts are, the better the
chance people will actually put them into action. So forget
the layers and all the different areas of your life you want to
look at for now. I'm going to ask you two simple questions.

What's draining you?

and

What's filling you up?

Bringing these questions into your body, what's constrict-ing you? What's expanding you? What tightens your shoul-ders? What opens your heart? What or who is currently sucking away your energy, rocking you off-center, stripping you of joy, and disconnecting you from yourself and your truth? And what or who is filling you up, giving you energy, promoting a sense of calm and centeredness, producing joy, and connecting you more to yourself and truth?

You can also think about it through the lens of frequen-cies. What or who is preventing you from living on a higher frequency (feeling love, curiosity, optimism, joy, gratitude, hope, the here and now—whatever expands you) and keep-ing you on a lower frequency in survival mode, in a panicked fight-or-flight state (feeling shame, hate, jealousy, judgment, anger, resentment—whatever constricts you)?

I'll go first.

Here are my current leaks—what's draining me, con-stricting me, keeping me living at lower frequencies:

Lopsided Friendships

Do you have friends who don't hit the ball back, don't return the call, don't show up the same in the friendship as you do? You give more time, energy, heart, to the friendship. You are always the one who has to text or call first. You're the first one at the restaurant. You're the one who's asking about their life and problems. They rarely ask about you. It feels like a one-way street.

We all have two types of friends. There are friends we are social with but don't go that deep with, and then there are what I call "coffee and crepe" friends. These are the friends we can truly be ourselves with, have life-changing conversations with, share our dreams and struggles with. With them, we experience the kind of connection that makes us feel like we don't need anyone else. But these days many of my "coffee and crepe" friends have drifted away. Or the friendships have become lopsided. They don't invest as much in them as I do. I often find myself over-extending to keep the friendship going, and that leaves me feeling drained.

We get things from friends that we can't get from our intimate partner. I used to file "friends" under "extra," assuming that when I had extra time and energy I'd spend it with my friends. Today I believe friends are essential, not extra. I file them now under "basic human needs." Good friends, the kind you want to grow old with, give you energy instead of draining it. I need more balanced friendship in my life.

Getting Older

I've never felt myself aging until this year. Before, age was just a number. Not anymore. Not when you have a child at forty-seven and you can see the height lines marked in her room inching higher as your wrinkles get deeper. You do the math and realize you will be Yoda's age by the time she's going to her senior prom. I see wrinkles on my face, and though I am trying to reframe them as tree rings, it's hard. I have been struggling with swimming toward fifty. I'm not as strong or as fast as I used to be. Whatever I eat I feel instantly. I don't wake up with boners anymore. But it's not the aging that's draining me. It's the rumination about it.

The Daily Stress and Energy Involved in Raising a Child

I'll be honest. Raising a child is ten times harder than I thought it would be. From the time I get up to when my head hits the pillow, I feel the constant pull to be present combined with all the to-dos just to keep the day moving. Life is no longer about me or my partner. It's about this other person. If day care gets canceled for whatever reason, my day goes down the drain. I scramble and can't work out or write or do the things I need to get done. The day falls apart, and I feel frustrated and behind. It puts me in a bad mood, and of course that impacts my relationship with my partner.

Future Tripping/Waiting for the Phone to Ring

Like everyone else, I struggle with cognitive distortions. The big one for me is future tripping. I get obsessed about things that haven't happened yet. I worry that my business deals won't come off and my partnerships will end. That I will lose my audience. That I won't be able to pay off my student loans and other debt. I worry that the phone will stop ringing.

Future tripping keeps me at a lower frequency, in an underlying state of worry and panic. Although it's not a giant leak—like it used to be before I had built anything—it can still drown me. Because stretched over time, future tripping can gray you out. The pattern of investing time and energy into something that hasn't happened yet can act like a virus that, for many people, literally makes them sick. I know I struggle with my future tripping the most at night, right before bed. It hijacks my sleep. And losing sleep then affects my mood, attitude, and quality of life the next day. If it continues, it also impacts my testosterone levels, with impacts on my workouts, and so on. My physiology begins to change. Future tripping is a leak I need to plug.

Now let's talk about what's filling me up these days. There's actually a lot. And notice that they're not big things that require money.

My Daughter

As much work and energy as it takes to raise a child, it is also extremely rewarding. I get to see the world through fresh new eyes. Discover new things I don't remember discovering myself, like how to peel an orange. Being a father at forty-eight grounds me and forces me to be mindful and present. It brings me joy daily. It fills me up.

Dirt Bikes

I've had street bikes for the past decade, but dirt bikes are new for me. I've wanted one since the '80s. All the cool kids had them. My parents bought me a little red Honda Spree 50cc scooter because they thought riding in the dirt with full gear and a helmet was more dangerous than riding a scooter on the street in flip-flops and with a grudge. Dirt bikes let me be twelve again. Playing in the sandbox and taking sweet jumps like the other kids. It fills me up.

Fitness

My fitness isn't what it used to be. The days of two-and-a-half-hour training sessions and making top three on the leaderboard are long gone. I'm definitely not as strong or as fast as I used to be. And I've struggled with that. But I've also finally changed what fitness looks like for me as I swim toward fifty. I'm now exploring new ways of staying fit, being kinder to myself, and trying to have more fun instead of trying to look better naked. My new relationship with fitness has allowed me to finally let go of the past, lean into new definitions, and find more joy in movement. It fills me up.

My Relationship with My Partner and with My Family

This is the first time in my life I have the picket fence: a home (not just a house) and a child with my partner. These two foundational layers have deepened my relationship with my partner in ways I've never experienced before. This anchor, this safe tree I come back to every day, reshuffles what's important and makes me work harder. Teaches me to rust. Gives me blinders and pure 92-octane heart fuel. Love feels very healthy these days. My partner and I seem to have both swum past the breakers—not just our own personal issues but also the conflicts and struggles of our relationship. It's the first time in a long time I've felt this calm in love. Like that moment when you light the candle, turn off the spigots filling the tub, and slide down into the water with your eyes closed and thinking about absolutely nothing. It fills me up.

My Purpose and Passion—Helping Others and Getting to Where I'm at in My Career

I'm still doing what I've been doing for the past thirteen years. But my reach has grown. I write books now. I have a podcast and have been doing some TV work, which is all new to me. Someone recognized me on the street the other day, and I was about to say *I'm not John Cho* (*Harold & Kumar*) when she said, "Are you John Kim?" I've spent most of my life as the basement guy—staring at a screen and hoping I'm making some kind of dent in the world. But these days I finally feel like I have come out of my room in the basement. As though the decade of blogging has manifested into a real career, and I'm not an almost guy anymore. It fills me up.

Spending More Time with My Mom

I used to work with my mom when we had a family restaurant-bar in Hollywood twenty years ago, pre-divorce, pre-rebirth, pre-"angry." After that I'd see her only on holidays or special occasions. But these days I see her once a week. She babysits our daughter for a couple of hours so we can go work out. These "practical" visits have turned into meaningful ones for me. It's hard to get my mom out of her house. She's one of those people who enjoys doing nothing. She doesn't like to eat out, and she doesn't like to go on trips. She likes her Korean dramas and staying inside. So it's just been nice, even if it's only once a week for a couple of hours, to see her face and buy her arepas and garlic yucca fries from a local food truck—the only outside food she actually loves. It fills me up.

The good news is that I have more filling me up than draining me. It hasn't always been like this. Most of my life has been spent trying to fix leaks. I wasn't happy with who I was or where I was at. I felt like the kid who got held back, twice, and I didn't have much that fulfilled me, save for a motorcycle and a gym membership. I felt constantly drained and lived mostly in my head in two states—worry and dread. That put me into a chasing state instead of an attracting one. I was lined with desperation and felt lost in the world. So of course I only put more pressure on myself to find someone to love.

Make a list of what's draining you these days and a list what's filling you up. What do you think about these two lists? Are there any surprises there? Does looking at all the things that are draining you make sense of how you've been feeling? Write down some action steps you can take to start plugging the leaks.

Rebuilding Your Big Life Pie Pieces

Now let's go a bit wider. Let's look at all your important life pie pieces. You have to decide what parts of your life are currently important to you. Some may be important to you now that weren't before your divorce. And vice versa.

Out of all the types of breakups, divorce is the sharpest double-edged sword. On one side, it may feel like your life is over. Because you may have lost everything you built and now have to start over. But on the other hand, a divorce can free you to build an entirely new life. It can be the catalyst to reevaluate everything, not just who you loved. Yes, other breakups can be similar catalysts. But a new life is the yolk of this egg. Once it's cracked, the yolk spills out.

And this can be the silver lining with divorce—afterward you have a new life. This is why so many (myself included) look back years later, after the dust has settled, and feel grateful for their divorce. Not only did they build a new life, but they became different people. The divorce made them look at themselves, at their wiring, behavior, and wounds, at their story, and then go on an inward journey.

The natural process of divorce prompts us to reevaluate all areas of our lives. It's the organic ripple from inside-out change. We start asking ourselves big questions, questions we've never asked before. Maybe because we were too scared. What if the answers called for life changes that the marriage didn't allow? Questions like:

Does my career fulfill me or am I doing this job only for the paycheck? Who are my real friends? Do I need to make new ones? Do I want to travel? Do I want to move to a new city?

What new passions do I want to invest in? Or reinvest in? When I'm ready, what kind of love experience do I want next? What would be good for me? How would I show up differently, because I'm different now? What makes me feel alive?

For me, these were the big life pie pieces I needed to focus on and build after my divorce:

New Friends and Community

I started to make new friends by taking fitness classes daily that already had a built-in community. I also told myself that I would not say no to any social invites. This got me out of my house and engaging with people I already had something in common with. I'm an introvert, so it was hard for me to get excited about going to barbecues and meetups. But I didn't break the promise to myself and always said yes to invites. Forced to be social, I met new people and heard their stories. It helped me get out of my own story.

Career and a Sense of Purpose

After my divorce, I decided to pursue a different career entirely. I was done with spending my days in coffee shops trying to come up with clever dialogue and "high-concept" story lines in the hopes that someone would buy it. I loved the art of writing, but it wasn't rewarding anymore. I was writing from desperation, not from creative expression. I was sick and tired of living with my fingers crossed and my happiness dependent on the phone ringing. I needed to do something more purpose driven. I wanted to be of service.

I built the career I have now by going back to school at age thirty-five to get my master's degree. Followed by a long journey of getting practicum hours and building a private practice.

A New Identity

I was known as Julie's husband. I had no other identity. I was the guy with the supper club (a family business that we sold) and the hot blond. That was it. That was my identity. I didn't know who I was. I didn't have a sense of self. So after the divorce I started building my identity by working on my character and values. I made my identity less about what I did for a living and more about how I showed up in the world. This started to build not only my character but, more importantly, a better relationship with myself. Simply put, I started to like myself. Then I asked: *How can I be of service and help others?* That's when I found my cape.

A New Mindset

It was easy for me to feel like a victim—like my wife had left me for no reason and life had dealt me some shitty cards. *There was nothing I could do. This is my life. I'm just white-knuckling my way through it.* But obviously that only kept me stuck inside a prison of my own making. So I started to reframe things.

First, I thought of my marriage as having expired. As I mentioned earlier, I reframed it as having been meant not to last a day longer or end a day sooner than it did. Then I imagined turning some dials in my mind to change my orientation. From judgment to wonder. From scarcity to abundance. From hate to love. And so on. I started to put action behind these reframings, and I built a new mindset that changed how I saw my situation. Going from having a fixed mindset to a growth mindset impacted all areas of my life. I went from feeling disempowered to empowered, and my life started to change.

A New Body (and a New Relationship with My Body)

In high school and college, I went to the gym often, but only for aesthetic reasons. I was trying to grow biceps and a chest like the other boys. I was insecure about my height and build, and my gym work was all for show, with zero connection to self. I never really had any kind of relationship with my body. Even with sex and intimacy, I'd use my body as a tool instead of being in my body. Sex was performative.

It wasn't until after my divorce that I started to establish a new relationship with my body. I did it through function fitness and my motorcycle. For the first time, my daily sweat was about movement and connecting to my body by being in it and pushing it as hard as I could. Not for abs, but for a sense of worth. Also, riding my motorcycle through the streets of LA and the canyons of Malibu grounded me. It was a meditation machine. It forced me to drop into my body and be super-present. I started to listen to my body more. Fed it good food and made sure it was hydrated. Asked it what it needed. Reminded myself to breathe and pay attention to my nervous system. For the first time in my life, I started to develop a relationship with my body.

A New Definition of Love and Happiness

My old definition of happy was money and success— the Range Rover–Porsche combo in the horseshoe-shaped driveway of a Spanish-style house in the Hollywood Hills and an office on a studio lot, with a three-picture deal. Happy was a glossy poster that had nothing to do with the quality of my inner life. My definition of love was the picket fence and happily ever after. I go down on you, you go down with me. I hung love on romance and sex and chemistry. Love was not built, but felt. Or not.

My happiness was tied to external things I had only so much control over, and love was a fresh romance novel with an unbroken spine. Today I believe happiness is an inner sanctuary created by our story and the quality of our relationship with self. It is crafted by the way we choose to see the world and how we can be of service. It comes in moments and is cumulative. Just like love. My definition of love today is that it is a daily choice and that it casts a black light on our wounds and reactions and things we need to look at to evolve and grow. Love is not a romance novel. It is a self-help book. That said, I still love Porsches and hot sex. And that's okay. Because those are things produced by me, not things that define me.

Slowly and daily, I started to build friends and community, a new career and sense of purpose, a new identity, a new mindset, and new relationships with my body and with self. I formed new definitions of love and happiness. This is how I started to build a new life—how I recovered from my divorce. I didn't go to Bali and have a spiritual awakening. I didn't shave my head and live in the mountains. I worked out, ate doughnuts, and rode my motorcycle. But I was conscious and intentional about my inner journey, which eventually manifested and rippled outward.

What would it look like for you to find new friends and community and build a new career and sense of purpose? To create a new identity, mindset, and relationship with your body? To come up with new definitions of love and happiness?

Write down what building out each of these areas would look like in your life. Would you reach out to friends you haven't been in contact with in a long time? Or someone you just met? Would you take new classes or courses to explore new passions? Would you pick up that guitar or a brush? Maybe put on your dancing shoes again?

How have you always identified yourself, and what is your current identity now that you're not married? What is your relationship with your body like? What do you want it to be? How do you want to feel in your body? What actions are needed to start building that feeling? What are your old definitions of love and happiness? Are they honest to you today? What would be some new definitions to explore? What would your life and decisions look like if you started to pull from new definitions?

Examine the Black Box

One of the most important steps to take after a relationship has expired is to examine the black box. Since marriage usually has a longer tail than other relationships, there's more to explore in order to change and bring something new to the table in your next relationship, such as the way you loved, the way you showed up, your unhealthy patterns, and the wounds that were activated and kept you reactive. The chances of having a new love experience, a corrective love experience, decrease exponentially if you let those patterns continue. But more than that, your evolution will be stunted. The growth soil is rich only if you examine how the plane went down and take ownership of your piece in it. Only if you resist the temptation to relive the story of your marriage by gaining the distance to examine self. Only if you examine the black box.

How do you examine the black box?

First, you have to be in a stable emotional place where you can look back and reflect without being activated. Otherwise, you may be sucked back into an emotional riptide. You have to get some distance. If just the thought of your ex drives you to punch holes in the wall, you are not there yet. This is why examining the black box is step 5 and not step 2. You don't want this step to bring things up before you're ready or you'll be ripping off scabs instead of learning about self and taking ownership, which is the greatest sign of growth.

How do you know if you're in an emotionally stable place?

There is no blanket answer. It's different for everyone. But here are some signs that you may be ready to examine the black box:

You can look back and not blame your ex for everything: Yes, he did some shitty things. Maybe he didn't have the ability to create a safe space, and that's why the relationship ended. But you finally see that it's not fair to blame him for everything that went wrong. There are things you did as well. Even if it was not speaking up or expressing your truth.

You don't want your ex dead: You actually wish her well and hope she has moved on and is happy.

You see your ex as a struggling human being like everyone else: Their goal in life isn't to make your life miserable. They are not out to hurt or destroy you. Even if they literally are, you don't see them that way. Not anymore. They're no longer a monster to you.

You realize you had a part in the plane going down: You finally see and acknowledge that you contributed to the ending. Not just the wobbles in the relationship but the actual crash. Even if you weren't the one who ended it, you were a copilot.

Not only do you realize that you had a part in the plane going down, but you want to work on your unhealthy patterns: Simply put, you want to take ownership by changing. Not for anyone else but yourself and the person you choose to invest in next. Because that person will be directly impacted by who you are when you meet them. The combination of the two of you will determine whether or not you have a new and different love experience. Because working on your unhealthy patterns will impact not only your growth but the growth of your next partner, you see it as your personal responsibility to work on yourself.

If some of the above (doesn't have to be all of it) resonates with you and you feel like you're in a good and stable place, here are some areas to look at. Think of them as doors into exploration of self. Walk through all of them.

DOOR—What are the main unhealthy patterns in your relationships? Where do those unhealthy patterns come from? Your story? Your childhood? Your previous relationships? How have those unhealthy patterns affected your relationships? What would it look like to fix, heal from, and change those unhealthy patterns?

DOOR—How do you handle conflict? How does handling conflict that way affect your relationships? What do you need to change about yourself and your way of handling conflict? What's getting in the way of executing that change? How can you dissolve those barriers?

DOOR—How do you communicate in relationships? Do you express yourself or do you hold things in? If you hold things in, how does that affect the relationship? How does that affect your relationship with yourself? How does your relationship with yourself affect your relationship with someone else? When you communicate, are you pulling from love and curiosity or from blame and judgment?

DOOR—What fears keep you emotionally distant and prevent intimacy? Where do those fears come from? What's one thing you can do to start overcoming those fears? What are you most afraid of about your relationship? How are those fears getting in the way of building the relationship? What about the relationship with yourself?

DOOR—What anger and resentment have you held on to in relationships? How does holding on to that resentment manifest in the relationship? What can you do to start letting go of the anger and resentment? Can you do that as a practice and use it as an active relationship tool while in the next relationship? Who do you need to forgive? What would happen if you didn't let go of the anger and resentment you're holding on to? How would letting go impact your own quality of life?

When You Feel Regret and Get Hard on Yourself

When examining the black box, feelings will come up. You can feel regret and start to blame yourself for things. So I want to remind you that you did the best you could with where you were at. Whatever you regret or blame yourself for is not a reflection of who you are as a person or of how hard you loved. Or didn't love. If you couldn't execute, it wasn't because you didn't want to, but because you didn't have the tools to do so. Would you get mad at yourself for not being able to run a triathlon if you've never trained for it? You may think, *Yes, I can run, ride a bike, and swim.* But swim half a mile, bike for 12.4 miles, and run for 3.1 miles, one right after the other? Of course you wouldn't get mad at yourself. Because exercising at this level is foreign to most of us.

Being in a relationship or marriage is not something we have trained for. Neither do we train for ending one. So whether you wanted out or your partner did, the breakup is always a surprise. Even if it wasn't. There was no practicing ahead of time how to dissolve a relationship. No fire drill. No steps taken that led to breakup. Only a loud voice saying that we could have or should have saved it. Or maybe that we should have ended it sooner. Both messages are harmful. Both create regret, blame, and shame.

The more you accept that you couldn't save the relationship, or that you shouldn't have ended it sooner, the better able you'll be to let go of regret. You can't blame yourself for who you were and the abilities you didn't have at the time. Sure, maybe now in looking back, whether ten years later or last summer, it's easy to say you should have done this or that. But at the time you were not who you are today. So it's unfair to say you should have done one thing or another. Because you could not have.

Regret can keep you stuck and spinning. It's easy to be angry at yourself. *Why didn't I end things when I knew, when I told my therapist it was over and I was finally going to have the conversation? When the relationship wasn't honest to me anymore after I'd tried so many times to fix it? When I noticed I had started breaking up with myself? Why did I wait so long? Not only did it affect my life, but it affected his too. It's my fault. I wish I was stronger. I wish I wasn't so scared.*

Write down all your regrets from the expired relationship. Then, next to each regret, write down a reframing of it. What came out of that regret that was actually good? What did you learn? How did it change you in a positive way? How did it reposition your life? What good things wouldn't have happened if what you regretted hadn't happen?

The Three-Step Reflection Technique

1. *Acknowledge:* Take a moment to acknowledge and label the regret you're feeling. Try saying to yourself, *I'm feeling regret about [specific situation].*

2. *Learn:* Reflect on what you've learned from the situation. Consider what actions you might take differently in the future and the lessons you've learned.

3. *Release:* Imagine placing your regret in a container, like a balloon, or in a river. Then watch it float away or flow downstream. Allow yourself to let go of the emotional weight associated with the regret.

Reminder

When one door closes, another door opens, but we look so long at the closed door that we don't see the one that has been opened for us.

Repeat—Turn Your Healing into a Lifestyle

Going through the three steps is not a onetime process. Like going to the gym or your meditation practice, you thread the steps into your daily life if you want to see results. Don't worry. You won't be doing this for the rest of your life, only during this chapter of your life. **But this chapter of your life will affect the rest of your life.** The work you put in now will reposition, realign, and set you up for irreversible secondary change.

This is the important piece, and something many do not consider or think about. Unlike physical change, internal change cannot be reversed. Yes, you can snap back at times, but when you turn working on yourself into a lifestyle there is a cumulative evolution. You reach a tipping point. The change cement dries. You are forever different, and your breakup was the catalyst to making that happen.

By threading these steps into your daily life, you're creating a new lifestyle:

Reframe your breakup as an expiration (accepting)
Cut the cord (drawing healthy boundaries)
Know that you are grieving (going through the stages of grief)
Do a life audit (realignment)
Examine the black box (owning your part in the breakup)
Repeat (turning your healing into a lifestyle)

Yes, there's a lot here, and it can feel overwhelming. That's why it's *not* something you tackle over the weekend.

Take it in daily bite-size chunks, building toward change. Remind yourself that your relationship has expired when you feel that tug and start playing back the highlight reel. Draw boundaries when it's hard to. Know you are grieving from a loss. Audit your life to stay aligned. Return to the crash and take ownership of your contribution so you can grow and learn from the experience and bring more to the next one. Stop hitting pause on your life and waiting for big things to happen or the next person to come along. Instead, find life in all the things you already have now and hit play. This is your new way of life.

So ask yourself, what does this look like? Answering the following questions will help you get started:

How often do you need to reframe your relationship? What does it look like to cut the cord? How do you grieve? What does that process look like in your daily life? What does it look like to realign your life? What kind of life inventory do you need to take? What do the steps look like? What does a life audit look like? Do you have to shift energy and investment with certain friends? How do you incorporate examining the black box into your lifestyle? How often do you need to do it and why? How do you find life in your life every single day?

Once You Get the Kite Airborne

After you've consistently threaded these foundational stages into your life and the tracks are laid—with structure and routine becoming guardrails, acceptance starting to cement, and revelations about self, love, and your past relationship bubbling up—you don't have to run so hard with the kite anymore. This means the heavy lifting is done and the wind of momentum will carry you. You can now take a breath and start spinning some other plates to keep the kite in the sky.

Forgive Yourself

We have all acted in ways we are not proud of and ways we regret. We have loved soft. We've drifted and checked out. We've cheated, blamed, and manipulated. We've run, numbed, and ignored. But we have to forgive ourselves or the anger turned inward will puncture our self-worth. Without forgiveness, we don't like ourselves, and that creates a disconnection that stunts our growth instead of promoting it. Remember, forgiveness is a process, not a light switch, and it's different for everyone. So don't judge your process. Also remember that forgiveness is a daily choice. Some days are hard. Some days are easy. Be patient and kind with yourself. Self-forgiveness is required to grow.

Build Self-Efficacy by Focusing on What You Can Control

Many of us let our lives revolve around our relationship. Especially over time. So the ending of one can feel like the floor just dropped out. We can feel like our life is falling apart and out of control. The house that was our life has crumbled. And that can produce feelings of panic, uncertainty, and hopelessness. But those are feelings. Not truth. To see more clearly and feel like you have control of your life again, that you have the ability to build and rebuild, create and accomplish, you have to focus on what you can control.

Focusing on what you cannot control will only make the walls slippery.

Here are some things you don't have control over:

Your ex's feelings

Your ex's behavior

What happened

How the relationship ended

How you could have loved

How your ex or other people feel about you and the expired relationship

Who your ex chooses to love next and when

How your friends or your ex's friends choose to see what happened

How your ex's friends behave toward you

How long it will take you to grieve the relationship and rebuild

You Will See Things You Didn't See Before (New Opportunities)

There may be things you see now that you couldn't see before. Or maybe you saw them but turned away. Love can create blinders. But the ending of the relationship gives you new lenses. You can see things that light you up and make you feel alive. And maybe they're right under your nose. But you also have to be open to seeing new things. Both your eyes and your mind have to be open. To give yourself new experiences pursue things you may not have had time for or were afraid to explore. Dance even if it's scary. Get curious about what's on the other side. Explore your passions, abilities, creativity, sexuality, spirituality, fears. There is no better time than now. Stretch. Yourself.

Seek Out Positive Experiences, Things, and People

First, how do you define "positive"? My definition is simple: Anything that expands you. That's it. And don't just *think* about what might be positive—drop into your body and *feel* it. That's how you truly know. Your heart, soul, energy, mind—do you feel yourself expanding?

So take a beat. Drop into your body. Does the new pursuit—a person, decision, experience, idea—expand you or constrict you? If it constricts you, it's negative. Now, can something be positive but constrict you because of your own anxiety, insecurities, and fears? Sure. And this is what you have to decipher. A good question to ask yourself is, *Does this feeling of constriction give me an opportunity for growth?* If you sit with it long enough and you're honest with yourself, you will know.

Embody Gratitude

Everyone says, "Practice gratitude." It's become a bumper sticker. A box to check off on a checklist. Over time practicing gratitude this way loses its impact because instead of actually taking a minute and feeling gratitude in our bones, we run a list in our head. Gratitude should be embodied, felt, noticed. As a return to something greater than self that leaves you holding God's hand. To embody gratitude means to shed ego, go beyond even acceptance, and connect the dots in your story. You can't do that when you're looking through human eyes. You must connect to your spirit. Turn yourself into a conduit. Allow gratitude to flow through you. Daily.

Make Value-Based Decisions That Line Up with Your Story

What matters to you and how does it line up with your story? If it matters to you but doesn't line up with your story, then you're most likely on the verge of making a bad decision. Pass on it. Respectfully. That decision won't hold weight or worth. Your story is gold and what truly matters is always tied to it, so your decisions have to line up with it. The way you contribute to other people's value is to make value-based decisions in your own life so that you have value. Otherwise, you will have nothing to give.

Smash the Clock

Don't judge yourself on how long it's taking you to get past the expiration of the relationship. Don't compare the time it took last time to how long it's taking this time, or how long it took your best friend or ex. Every expired relationship is different. You are different. Each of us is unique. A single serving. So give yourself time, space, and compassion. Healing doesn't have a timeline.

The Other Clock

You're not getting too old to have babies, start a family, buy a house, or do whatever you want to do for yourself. If your body can't produce a child, there are other options. You also don't need a partner to have a child or a family. We have been programmed by society's timelines and shoulds. But the secret is that you're going to age and grow regardless of whether or not, or when, you hit your milestones. Would you rather compromise to hit age marks and fall into old patterns or build something honest and sustainable when you're ready?

I went back to school at age thirty-four.

I got divorced at age thirty-five.

I did my first back squat at age thirty-six.

I sold my first book at age forty.

I had a child at age forty-seven.

TWO TRUTHS TO CLEAR UP MISCONCEPTIONS

I want to offer two truths about breakups that have helped me tremendously. I have purposely placed them at the end of the book instead of the beginning because I want them to linger with you. I want you to let them sink in. They have been game changers for me, and I continue to remind myself of them daily.

I didn't learn these truths in therapy school or from self-help books. They came from my own self-discovery journey as well as from the clients I have helped throughout the years. They represent mindsets, something I keep in my back pocket. When I remind myself of these two truths, I am able to pull back, see the bigger picture, connect the dots, and make sense of things. These two truths will help you let go, reframe, rediscover, empower yourself, and change the way you see your breakup.

It Was Never About the Promise

So many want the promise. So many crave a contract. So many want a guarantee.

But love is not property or an investment, like it was up until the '50s. Love is also not an image to project to the world—the image of a perfect life behind a picket fence, raising 2.2 kids and baking pies but walking on eggshells. Living a dishonest life for its presentation value.

Love is space. And in that space, a belief is born. Around that belief, the action of love is wrapped. Like arms. And that action, assuming it's healthy, protects the space where the belief—the love—continues to grow and evolve. Or doesn't. But it's not about love being locked in or tied to the future, something we can never guarantee. Yes, knowing we'll be together forever would make us feel safe. But would it? Because it's a lie.

If you focus on the intention, the expansion, the possibilities, the something greater that comes from two whole people growing together, and less on the deal, the agreement, and all the what-ifs, you will be more accepting if the relationship doesn't feel honest to you and does end. Acceptance, our underestimated superpower, will come from seeing love as a living, breathing thing rather than as something to be captured. Acceptance doesn't live in matching rings and official ties. It lives in pure presence. Feeling free is what makes you feel love because love is fueled by the ability to choose, daily, one day at a time. Not promising to love every day for the rest of your life. That's not love. That's a lie. No one can promise you that. It's not the commitment that bears fruit, but the learning and sharing of life, the ups and downs and sideways, the collisions of the exchange.

I, like you, have put the promise first. I, like you, have grabbed before holding. And I, like you, have lost.

Engagement holds new meaning today. It's not a ring on a finger. It's not about locking anything down. It's about being fully present and seen, about hard conversations, about awareness and ownership, with transparency, connection, and a respectful distance. Championing your story, not just your chapter. Looking beyond the skin and loving with eyes closed and palms open. It's no longer about the picket fence. Because we all know that shit has splinters.

I, like you, have loved with only my eyes. I, like you, exchanged vows for security and a false permanence as a way to control. And I, like you, have lost.

There is so much more to love than what we see. The superglue is produced not only in how the connection makes us feel but in what we learn about ourselves through it. The space that two souls create as both walk through life together. Getting lost. Then found. Lost. Found. Together. Turbulence and the underbelly create the glue, not the "happily ever after" we all bought into. That's sugar. Empty calories.

The thing is, we can't undo what happened that led to a breakup. Attraction, healthy or not, is real. We liked what we liked. We were who we were. Now the cement is dry. That chapter is closed. But we can give it less power by putting weight on new things. Like what we learned and who we became.

Every Part of Your Story Will Be Used

We all want to rip out chapters and erase parts of our story that recall shame, guilt, and regret. I get it. I've wanted to delete my divorce more than anything in my life. Rip out the ten years I spent alone, feverishly punching keys in coffee shops to become a screenwriter. I've wished I could erase the club days in Hollywood from my twenties, when I exchanged my truth for membership and chased tinsel. I've wished I could erase every shitty job where I wore wrinkle-free pants and hid in the restroom until they found me. And that one time I was hired to be the travel sober coach for a high-profile client who lied and went missing. So many times in my life I felt that I had failed. So many chapters on which I wish I could hit delete all:

Divorce: Divorce forced me to cross that great divide from boy to man, from child to adult. It was the greatest catalyst for growing up and building my own life. But more importantly, it led to building a relationship with myself. For the first time in my life. It gave me a reason to start a blog, a community, a full practice to work in a way that was honest to me, with freedom and purpose.

Failed screenwriter: A decade of sitting in coffee shops pumping out screenplays as fast as I could (ten pages a day) trained me to write fast and efficiently. Those days taught me how to turn writing into a lifestyle. Without that experience, I couldn't have written five thousand blog posts after my divorce that laid the tracks on which I knock out a book a year these days.

Club guy: Turning our family's restaurant into a scenic super club was what allowed my mom to retire and me to finally step away from the family business, which I'd been stuck working in since I was a teen. The crash and burn of the club freed me. It gave me permission to go back to school and become a therapist.

Shitty clinical jobs: All the shitty clinical jobs where I was underpaid and overworked created the drive in me to build something of my own. Those jobs drove me to pursue my passions with a sense of purpose. They also put a fire in my belly to help others build their practices and their work in ways that were honest to them as well.

Client AWOLing: I was humbled when clients disappeared. That made me realize that helping people doesn't always have a happy ending. I can't save people. I don't have the answers. I can be wrong. I'm not for everyone. And I can only meet my clients where they are. I remind myself of this regularly to this day.

Your story is the most valuable thing you will ever own. And it will be your legacy. Stories are all about the setups and payoffs. What you went through (the setups) and are going through now (more setups) will pay off later. Most likely in ways you, like me, never imagined. And it's this setting up and paying off process that creates journeys, character arcs, and eventually your evolution.

Those chapters of your life that you want to rip out are crucial. Because without them, there are no payoffs. There is no unfolding. Your story runs flat. The value is lost. To grow and evolve, you must use all parts of your story.

Conclusion

We are all loving beings who started with honest hearts and good intentions. Our not so loving side comes out in the presence of pain, protection, and fear. You didn't dodge a bullet when a relationship ended, because there was a takeaway for you in what happened, and for the person you loved. And every takeaway is gold, offering you life and love lessons that you wouldn't have had otherwise. Most of the time those lessons aren't obvious, and you don't take them in until later. Sometimes much later.

We get different things, both healthy and unhealthy, from everyone we love. Some love leaves us with information, some reminds us of what we don't want and what doesn't work, and some holds up a mirror. But it's all learning, about self, life, and our love journey. If you see expired relationships as time wasted, whether they lasted for one date or a rocky seven years, you will harbor anger and resentment that closes your heart and narrows your human capacity. More importantly, you will stop believing.

If you stop believing, the chances that you will find love flatten like a tire over spikes. And what you bring to the table in your next experiences will be flat love. Guarded and hopeless. Re-creating old love experiences instead of being rewired for something new. At the end of the day, it's a choice.

There was no bullet to dodge. Only two people who collided and then took away lessons and insights about love and self and what they wanted next. But most importantly, they tried—with everything they had, from where they were in their lives. Because that's what life and love are about. The attempt. There is more courage in the attempt to show up, to give, and to receive than there could ever be in something that isn't honest.

You tried, and that was enough.

Break Up on Purpose Mixtape

Usually we make mixtapes to show love. Why can't we make one to heal from expired love? Below are a few songs I had on repeat on many of my breakup journeys. Listening while ditching work and running on the beach. A night ride on my motorcycle. Doing laundry. Cleaning my apartment. Going on long walks. Sipping overpriced pour-over coffee and people-watching. I hope you make yourself your own mixtape, to listen to while you're doing whatever you're doing to get out of your house and out of your head.

"I Found You"—Alabama Shakes
I've gone on many runs listening to this song. I'm not sure who the songwriter has in mind when she sings "I finally found you." I'm assuming the person she loves. But for me, I saw myself. I finally found myself. The lyrics actually become more powerful if you apply them to you finally finding you. "Traveled a long way and it took a long time to find you, but I finally found you." Try listening but thinking about finally finding you, instead of a love.

"California"—Delta Spirit

One of my exes moved to California after we'd been dating long distance. She said it wasn't for me. I believe she moved here for us. After I abruptly ended the relationship, and feeling a tremendous amount of guilt, I discovered this song and wished I could send it to her. "I want you to move to California for yourself. I want you to find whatever your heart needs."

"Lovely Day"—Bill Withers

When he says "Then I look at you," the YOU is not a person. It's life, the universe, the blade of grass growing through cracked concrete. YOU is sun on your back and a gas tank in between your legs while watching the sun set. YOU is New York–style pizza and a meaningful conversation with a friend. YOU is hope and closure and all the possibilities this life has to offer. And you can still have a lovely day. Single.

"I Will Survive"—Cake

There's something about Cake's version of this song that just hits different. Maybe a man singing was a reminder that men can also feel pain, fear, lost, and angry. This was my anthem for many of my expired relationships: "I've got all my life to live, I've got all my love to give." Yes, a great reminder that love doesn't run out. And I will continue on with my life. Building one day at a time. I will survive.

"How's It Going to Be"—Third Eye Blind

This was one of my first breakup songs. I was in my twenties and it was my first real relationship, which lasted three years. Although she's the one who ended it, I had an inner calm of acceptance, like the ringing of the end-of-the-day school bell. No devastation. No anger, hate, or regrets. Just a knowing that it's time to let go. Two high school kids accepting they're going to separate colleges. A pure sadness. A clean sadness. Every time I hear this song, it reminds me that breakups don't have to be ugly. It takes me back to a simpler time, an innocent time, when codependency was cute and we didn't have to label everything. When you could say something and take it back and there would be no consequences. When love was young. And our hearts were powdered snow.

"Change"—Tracy Chapman
This one is a gripper. Of course, it's Tracy Chapman. I've wept uncontrollably listening to this in my car many times. What's powerful about this song is it brought it all back to me and my contribution to the expiration. It made me think about what I needed to change about myself. What were my shortcomings? What did I need to take ownership for? She asks what it would take, how bad or how good things need to be, for you to make changes. The question is would this breakup make you change? I hope it does.

"Wishing Well"—The Airborne Toxic Event
Blasting this song as I cut through the canyons of the Hollywood Hills to get to work on my first Ducati 620 motorcycle. It was my first bike. I had just found CrossFit. I felt invincible. It was the first time in my life I felt solitude instead

of loneliness. Also, there's an Asian guy in this band. Fuck yeah.

"Never Tear Us Apart"—The Horrible Crowes

This song always reminds me of young love. When love was sticky, possessive, and delusional. When we lost ourselves in each other because that's what we thought it meant to love with everything. It makes me reflect and see why it didn't work out. They didn't tear us apart. We tore each other apart. Because we didn't have the tools. Listening to this song helped me remind myself of that.

"Bad Love"—Dehd

The way I interpreted this song was to run from the old and lean into the new. "New love baby, come on, honey, gimme some." "Some" would be the new love experience. I would literally be running while listening to this song, imagining myself shedding the old versions of me and imagining what new love could look like, feel like. It gave me fuel to know I was running with direction. Not chasing, but rather becoming.

"Everybody's Changing"—Keane

This was playing on the stereo in our SUV while we were looking out at the ocean. Santa Barbara was supposed to be a romantic getaway but ended up being the weekend I knew was the beginning of the end. We didn't say a word. Just both stared straight ahead listening to Keane, and I remember feeling like she was outgrowing me. Even though we were sitting right next to each other, it was the first time she didn't defend her distance. And that's how I knew. "Everybody's changing and I don't know why." A few months later, she wanted a separation, which quickly turned into a divorce. Since then I've played this song during other breakups, because sometimes we need to listen to an old song that reminds us of a different breakup. It makes us remember who we were and how far we've come. Songs can act as measuring sticks. Because since that day in the parking lot of the beach, I've never felt held back again. That "everyone's changing and I don't know why." Because I am changing as well.

"Oregon"—Tez Cadey

This song has no words. And that's what I love about it. It starts slow and builds to a crescendo, the perfect visualization song. I've lain on the floor of my Los Feliz apartment so many Friday nights seeing who I wanted to become while blasting this song. To feel in my bones as if things have already happened. As if I was already there. It always took me to a spiritual place. An out-of-body experience. I still play this song often. It makes me feel close to God. It takes me to church.

"It Ain't Over 'Til It's Over"—Lenny Kravitz

When he says "It ain't over 'til it's over," I don't see it as the relationship he's referring to. I interpret it as the closure of the expiration. The whole thing. The journey and healing of the breakup is not separate from the breakup.

When I interpret it that way, it reminds me to keep working on healing. It ain't over until I find closure and forgiveness (including with self). "So much time wasted. Playing games with love. So many tears I've cried. So much pain inside." Just because the relationship is over doesn't mean the work is.

"Rise Up"—Andra Day

This song reminds me of the sun. An anthem to stand each day. On the days you don't feel like getting out of bed. One pant leg at a time. One cup of coffee at a time. One controlled thought. One workout. One step. One day, at a time.

I'll rise up
I'll rise unafraid

"About Today"—The National

One of the saddest songs ever. It's simply about drift. Two people who drifted away and no one did anything about it. "Today, you were far away. And I didn't ask you why." What's so powerful about this song is that it doesn't talk about the whys. Just the drift. It's sad because it happens so often. It has happened in every one of my relationships. If not both of us, then one, which can be more damaging to the relationship due to the isolation. The kind of loneliness one can feel in a relationship is both common and crushing. This song reminds me that sometimes we realize that "being far away" can be the leaky faucet that can drown both of us. It makes me want to pay attention to any drift in future relationships and address them before people drift too far to come back.

"And I Fell Back Alone"—World Party

People walking through each other as they leave the room. Having no need to know each other anymore. For me, this song is about knowing it's over. When love tried all the right moves but the walls came down anyway. Waking up and realizing it wasn't just a fight this time. The silence finally broke the relationship. It's done. There is no more us. And I fall back alone. Sometimes sad songs that remind you it's really over are needed. Sometimes you need to sit in the bathwater.

"The Background"—Third Eye Blind

Although it may not be what the song's about, this song gave me permission to carry fond memories of expired love in the background. And there's a difference between the background and foreground. It didn't mean I wanted to get back together. You can play the highlight reel without wanting to watch the movie again. It just meant I could hold on to the memories for what they were instead of obeying society's "should" and ripping them out of my story. I don't think it's toxic or unhealthy to reminisce about someone you have loved. I get healthy boundaries and not playing the relationship back if you still want to be back. But if you have some closure and acceptance and zero interest in a round two, they're valuable life moments you can carry without judgment. Like childhood. I think it helps us let go, accept, and understand. I think when we force ourselves to not think about something, we think about it more. So allowing yourself to play things back when needed, when reminded, when it organically surfaces, is okay. "I carry you around, in the background."

"This Is the Day"—The The

This song reminds me that this may be the day. The day that something shifts inside. An insight, a revelation, a new decision. You don't have to win the lottery or meet someone new for it to be "the day." It can be subtle. Nuanced. Slight. And like a microadjustment of a golf swing, over time the ball can end up in an entirely new place. And sometimes, things don't hit you until it does. And this could be that day. Growth isn't linear. This song always gave me hope and a half smile. Because this could be the day that—

I notice the sun on my face.

I'm not in panic survival mode anymore.

I am able to be grateful for my life and story.

I do one more burpee.

I finish something.

Or start something.

I listen to my body.

I stop running from things.

I eat healthy.

I draw boundaries.

I sleep. Hard.

I smile.

I finally look inward.

I actually feel like myself. Again.

Resources

For short-form inspiration, reminders, and street-level concepts three times a week that have helped me through all my expired relationship journeys, check out *The Angry Therapist* podcast (more than eight hundred episodes and counting).

Also, if you want a daily dose texted to you every morning so you can wake up to a reminder, a new perspective, or a fresh mindset to help you with your day, get my daily texts at www.theangrytherapist.com.

Acknowledgments

First, thank you. For picking up this book or any of my books. For following me on social media, watching any of my videos, or listening to my podcast. During my divorce, you were the ones who helped me find my cape. You gave me a sense of purpose when I had no hope or direction. You helped me discover my voice and gave me the courage to share my story. You made me feel seen, heard, and understood, and that I had something to contribute to this world. Without you, I would still be a miserable fuck toiling away somewhere in a nondescript office with a tucked-in shirt and a phony smile, wishing I had the courage to help people in a way that felt more honest to me.

To Vanessa. For your support and belief in me. For championing my work. For watching our daughter so I could write. For redefining love and partnership. Thank you for being by my side through it all. There is no greater love than a partner willing to read all your drafts. You make me want to be a better writer.

To my assistant Tess, who fell from the sky. Thank you for

all your daily hard work throughout the years. For helping me keep all the balls in the air. For going above and beyond. For helping me help others. What a blessing you have been.

To Pilar, my agent. For looking out for me and my career. For listening to all my crazy ideas. For making me feel safe so I can just write. I sleep better with you on my team.

To the HarperOne team. We have danced together five times now. I am so grateful and honored to be in your stable of authors. To Sydney, Daniella, Shannon, and Maya for your eyes and contribution to this book. It was a long ride. Thank you for riding shotgun. To Lucile and Courtney, for all the years of helping me push all my books out into the world. Thank you for not making it feel like work.

Today's Listen

A special episode just for people who have purchased this book . . . from *The Angry Therapist* podcast.

Join me and my community of like-minded people all re-building themselves. We're not meant to do this alone. Hope to see you inside!